767
Sports Questions
Your Friends Can't Answer

THOMSON

PETERSON'S

Australia • Canada • Mexico • Singapore • Spain • United Kingdom • United States

THOMSON

PETERSON'S ™

About Thomson Peterson's
Thomson Peterson's (www.petersons.com) is a leading provider of education
information and advice, with books and online resources focusing on education
search, test preparation, and financial aid. Its Web site offers searchable databases
and interactive tools for contacting educational institutions, online practice tests and
instruction, and planning tools for securing financial aid. Thomson Peterson's serves
110 million education consumers annually.

For more information, contact Thomson Peterson's, 2000 Lenox Drive, Lawrenceville
NJ 08648; 800-338-3282; or find us on the World Wide Web at www.petersons.com/
about.

Editor: Wallie Walker Hammond; Production Editor: Teresina Jonkoski; Proofreader:
Bret Bollman; Manufacturing Manager: Ray Golaszewski; Composition and Interior
Design: Michele Able; Cover Design: Greg Wuttke.

ISBN-10: 0-7689-2458-8
ISBN-13: 978-0-7689-2458-9

Printed in Canada

9 8 7 6 5 4 3 2   07 06

First Edition

Contents

Introduction v

CHAPTER 1   Buy Me Some Peanuts and Cracker Jack: Baseball 1

CHAPTER 2   Goal Line Stand: Football... 19

CHAPTER 3   Drive to the Hoop: Basketball 37

CHAPTER 4   Off Its Moorings: Hockey.. 53

CHAPTER 5   Running on Full Throttle: Auto Racing 69

CHAPTER 6   The Galloping Ghost and Chocolate Thunder: Nicknames .. 85

CHAPTER 7   Hear Me Roar: Women in Sports... 101

CHAPTER 8   In the Bunker: Golf.. 117

CHAPTER 9   Serve and Volley: Tennis 133

CHAPTER 10 Going for the Gold: The Olympic Games 151

CHAPTER 11 On the Sidelines: Coaches 169

CHAPTER 12 A Plaque on the Wall: Hall of Famers 185

CHAPTER 13 The Sweet Science: Boxing.. 203

CHAPTER 14 The Ring's the Thing: Championship Teams...................... 219

CHAPTER 15 Hanging from the Rafters: Retired Numbers

             (and other famous jersey numbers)................................... 235

Introduction

767 Sports Questions Your Friends Can't Answer was written with one goal in mind: To have some fun. Really! And hey, after correctly answering the questions in this book, you'll be more than ready to impress your friends and family. Go ahead—challenge someone to a game of Trivial Pursuit™ or play along with *Jeopardy!™*. And the next time you get stuck with a bunch of sport snobs at some party, be confident that you can keep up with the conversation. Remember . . . your friends don't know all of the answers, but you do! Have some fun and good luck.

HOW WELL DO YOU KNOW YOUR SPORTS TRIVIA?

When you complete a chapter, use the answers that follow to check your responses. Here's a scoring key to grade yourself and see how you rate at sports trivia.

SCORING KEY

Give yourself two points for each correct answer.

90–100   *Excellent.* You are the master of sports knowledge.

80–89   *Good.* You have more than a passing knowledge of this subject.

70–79   *Fair.* You have a competent grasp of many aspects of this subject.

60–69   *Poor.* You could use some improvement in this area.

Below 60   *Time for sports trivia training.* Maybe you could start reading the sports pages more often!

CHAPTER 1

Buy Me Some Peanuts and Cracker Jack:
Baseball

1. A perfect game is defined as which of the following?

   (A) When a hitter reaches base in every at bat

   (B) When a pitcher pitches a complete game

   (C) When a pitcher pitches a complete game and gives up no hits and no walks

   (D) When a pitcher records every out with a strikeout

2. Who holds the record for the most career home runs?

   (A) Barry Bonds

   (B) Mark McGwire

   (C) Harmon Killebrew

   (D) Hank Aaron

> In Baseball, you don't know nothin'.
> —YOGI BERRA

3. Who holds the record for most career no-hitters with 7?

   (A) Cy Young

   (B) Steve Carlton

   (C) Roger Clemens

   (D) Nolan Ryan

4. Which of the following was the last stadium to have games played at night because it had no lights on the field?

   (A) Wrigley Field

   (B) Fenway Park

   (C) Yankee Stadium

   (D) Comiskey Park

5. Which of the following teams was once referred to as the "Big Red Machine"?

   (A) The Boston Red Sox

   (B) The Cincinnati Reds

   (C) The Texas Rangers

   (D) The California Angels

6. Who was the first American League pitcher to throw a perfect game?

   (A) Smokey Joe Wood

   (B) Don Larsen

   (C) Addie Joss

   (D) Cy Young

7. Members of the "40/40 Club" all can boast which of the following?

   (A) 40 home runs after the age of 40

   (B) 40 stolen bases after the age of 40

   (C) 40 home runs and 40 stolen bases in the same season

   (D) 40 wins in a season by the age of 40

8. Which of the following pitchers holds the records for most career wins, most career losses, and most career complete games?

(A) Sandy Koufax

(B) Walter Johnson

(C) Cy Young

(D) Christy Matthewson

9. Rickey Henderson holds which two career records?

(A) The most hits and most runs

(B) The most runs and most stolen bases

(C) The most hits and most stolen bases

(D) The most hits and most leadoff homers

10. Which team won the most World Series pennants in the twentieth century?

(A) New York Yankees

(B) Baltimore Orioles

(C) Brooklyn Dodgers

(D) Boston Red Sox

11. The 1919 Chicago White Sox are known as the "Black Sox" for which of the following reasons?

(A) They were the first team to wear black socks.

(B) They were the first team to be integrated.

(C) They were the first team to use black stripes under their eyes.

(D) They allegedly threw the World Series.

12. In which city is the Baseball Hall of Fame located?

(A) Canton

(B) Springfield

(C) Cooperstown

(D) New York City

13. Cal Ripken Jr. broke whose record for most consecutive games played?

    (A) Joe DiMaggio

    (B) Lou Gehrig

    (C) Mickey Mantle

    (D) Babe Ruth

14. Who is infamous for the "pine tar incident"?

    (A) Earl Weaver

    (B) Catfish Hunter

    (C) Pete Rose

    (D) George Brett

15. Who holds the single season record for saves?

    (A) John Smoltz

    (B) Bobby Thigpen

    (C) Lee Smith

    (D) Dennis Eckersley

16. Eddie Matthews played for the Braves in how many different cities?

    (A) 1

    (B) 2

    (C) 3

    (D) 4

17. Joe DiMaggio's streak of consecutive games with a hit lasted how many games?

    (A) 26

    (B) 36

    (C) 46

    (D) 56

18. Which of the following is a movie about a women's professional league?

   (A) *A League of Their Own*

   (B) *The Rookie*

   (C) *There's No Crying in Baseball*

   (D) *The Georgia Peaches Play Ball*

19. How many games are currently played in a complete major league season?

   (A) 62

   (B) 82

   (C) 162

   (D) 182

20. What is the battery?

   (A) A player who hustles all the time

   (B) The batter, the player on deck, and the player in the hole

   (C) The pitcher and the catcher

   (D) The three outfielders

21. Who holds the career record for batting average, with an amazing .367?

   (A) Ty Cobb

   (B) Ted Williams

   (C) Lou Gehrig

   (D) Tony Gwynn

22. Which pitching duo of brothers has the most career wins?

   (A) Jim and Gaylord Perry

   (B) Joe and Dom DiMaggio

   (C) Joe and Phil Niekro

   (D) Andy and Alan Benes

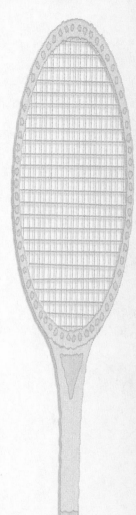

23. Home Run King Hank Aaron also holds which dubious record?

   (A) Most career strikeouts

   (B) Most career hits into double plays

   (C) Most career games missed due to injury

   (D) Most career ejections

24. To win the Triple Crown of hitting in baseball, a player must lead the league in which of the following?

   (A) Batting average, slugging percentage, and on-base percentage

   (B) Batting average, home runs, and RBIs

   (C) Doubles, triples, and home runs

   (D) Stolen bases, walks, and hits

25. To win the Triple Crown of pitching in baseball, a player must lead the league in which of the following?

   (A) Wins, losses, and saves

   (B) Wins, saves, and complete games

   (C) Wins, strikeouts, and complete games

   (D) Wins, strikeouts, and ERA

26. In 1983, Fred Lynn accomplished which All-Star Game feat?

   (A) He became the first and only player to hit for the cycle in an All-Star game.

   (B) He became the first and only player to hit a grand slam in an All-Star game.

   (C) He became the first and only player to play all nine positions in an All-Star game.

   (D) He became the first and only player to steal second, third, and home in an All-Star game.

27. Managers Casey Stengel and John McGraw share which of the following records?

    (A) Most championships

    (B) Fewest championships

    (C) Most career wins

    (D) Most different teams managed

28. The distance between the pitcher's mound and home plate is which of the following?

    (A) 45 feet

    (B) 45 feet 6 inches

    (C) 60 feet

    (D) 60 feet 6 inches

29. Babe Ruth hit the first home run in stadium history in which of the following ballparks?

    (A) Fenway Park

    (B) Yankee Stadium

    (C) Ebbets Field

    (D) Comiskey Park

30. Who holds the record for most RBIs in a season?

    (A) Lou Gehrig

    (B) Babe Ruth

    (C) Hack Wilson

    (D) Hank Aaron

31. Which pitcher holds the major league record for most consecutive scoreless innings pitched?

    (A) Don Drysdale

    (B) Walter Johnson

    (C) David Wells

    (D) Orel Hershiser

32. Which of the following is *not* considered a balk?

   (A) The pitcher, while touching the rubber, feints a throw to first base and fails to complete the throw.

   (B) The pitcher delivers the ball to the batter while he is not facing the batter.

   (C) The pitcher, without having the ball, stands on or astride the rubber or while off the rubber, he feints a pitch.

   (D) The pitcher attempts a throw to first base but the ball hits the baserunner.

33. In 1947, Jackie Robinson played for which team when he became the first African American player in the major leagues during the modern era?

   (A) Yankees

   (B) Dodgers

   (C) Braves

   (D) Giants

34. Who, in 1980, became the first major leaguer to earn $1,000,000 in a season?

   (A) Mike Schmidt

   (B) Dave Winfield

   (C) Reggie Jackson

   (D) Nolan Ryan

35. Of the following, which two teams entered the league as expansion teams in the same year?

   (A) Marlins and Devil Rays

   (B) Devil Rays and Rockies

   (C) Rockies and Diamondbacks

   (D) Diamondbacks and Devil Rays

36. A player who bats below .200 is said to be which of the following?

    (A) Playing with a hole in his bat

    (B) Batting like a girl

    (C) Hitting below the Mendoza Line

    (D) Acting like a buttercup hitter

37. When Chan Ho Park made his major league debut in 1994, he became the first player from which of the following countries to play in the majors?

    (A) Japan

    (B) China

    (C) Nepal

    (D) Korea

38. Of Hank Aaron's 755 career homers, how many were inside-the-park home runs?

    (A) 0

    (B) 1

    (C) 14

    (D) 27

39. Why was there "no joy in Mudville"?

    (A) Baseball's first work stoppage ended the season.

    (B) Mudville lost its first-ever baseball game.

    (C) Casey struck out.

    (D) Mudville lost its team to contraction.

40. Which position has the most players represented in the Hall of Fame?

    (A) Pitcher

    (B) Catcher

    (C) Right field

    (D) Shortstop

41. Who was the last person to win the Triple Crown of hitting?

(A) Mike Piazza

(B) Mike Schmidt

(C) Cal Yastrzemski

(D) Jimmie Foxx

42. Which of the following players once pitched 14 innings in a World Series game?

(A) Babe Ruth

(B) Cy Young

(C) Walter Johnson

(D) Joe Bush

43. Which of the following groups of players is tied with 24 All-Star appearances, the major league record?

(A) Hank Aaron, Babe Ruth, and Nolan Ryan

(B) Eddie Murray, Hank Aaron, and Willie Mays

(C) Stan Musial, Ted Williams, and Hank Aaron

(D) Hank Aaron, Stan Musial, and Willie Mays

44. Each year, Rolaids® presents an award to the best player in which of the following categories?

(A) The best infielder

(B) The best outfielder

(C) The best reliever

(D) The fastest-throwing pitcher

45. Which of the following was the most recent set of twins to play in the major leagues at the same time?

(A) Jose and Ozzie Canseco

(B) Ryan and Damon Minor

(C) Stew and Stan Cliburn

(D) Eddy and Johnny O'Brien

46. In major league history, only 11 unassisted triple plays have ever been recorded. Players at which of the following positions are responsible for the most unassisted triple plays?

    (A) Pitcher

    (B) First base

    (C) Second base

    (D) Shortstop

47. What was unusual about the home run that Tim Stoddard hit in 1986 in the last at bat of his career?

    (A) It was a grand slam.

    (B) It was an inside the park home run.

    (C) His brother was pitching.

    (D) It was the first of his career.

48. Who is the only player in history to throw consecutive no-hitters?

    (A) Cy Young

    (B) Johnny Vander Meer

    (C) Walter Johnson

    (D) Satchel Paige

49. Which of the following players holds the single season record for most times successfully stealing home?

    (A) Rickey Henderson

    (B) Lou Brock

    (C) Chuck Knoblauch

    (D) Ty Cobb

50. Which of the following teams can claim the most members of the Hall of Fame?

    (A) Giants

    (B) Yankees

    (C) Dodgers

    (D) Braves

51. Who was on deck when Bobby Thomson hit "The Shot Heard Around the World" off pitcher Ralph Branca?

    (A)   Dusty Rhodes

    (B)   Ron Noble

    (C)   Satchel Paige

    (D)   Willie Mays

52. Who hit his 700th home run on September 17, 2004?

    (A)   Mark McGwire

    (B)   Barry Bonds

    (C)   Sammy Sosa

    (D)   Rafael Palmeiro

CHAPTER 1 ANSWERS

1. **The correct answer is (C).** A perfect game occurs when a pitcher pitches a complete game and gives up no hits and no walks. It is one of the rarest of all baseball feats. Choice (B) is incorrect because a pitcher can complete a game yet still allow runs to score and even lose.

2. **The correct answer is (D).** Hank Aaron holds the career home run mark with 755 homers.

3. **The correct answer is (D).** Nolan Ryan holds the record for most career no-hitters with 7, which is several games ahead of the next pitcher on the list.

4. **The correct answer is (A).** Wrigley Field was the last of the stadiums listed as answer choices to add lights and play night games. Wrigley Field added the lights in 1988 and the first night game at Wrigley occurred on August 8 of that season.

5. **The correct answer is (B).** The 1975 and 1976 World Champion Cincinnati Reds were referred to as the Big Red Machine. The word "red" appears in choices (A) and (B), so that should help you narrow down your choices, if you're completely unsure. (Remember, if you can narrow the choices down to 2 out of 4, you increase your chances of getting the answer correct to 50 percent.)

6. **The correct answer is (D).** The first perfect game in American League history was thrown by Cy Young on May 5, 1904, when he led the Boston Red Sox to victory over the Philadelphia Athletes.

7. **The correct answer is (C).** A very elite club, the "40/40 Club" includes only those players who have hit 40 home runs and have 40 stolen bases in the same season.

8. **The correct answer is (C).** One of the reasons Cy Young holds all three of these records is that he has the most career pitching appearances, which is due mostly to the fact that pitchers often made 40–50 starts per season in his era.

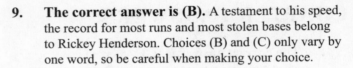

9. **The correct answer is (B).** A testament to his speed, the record for most runs and most stolen bases belong to Rickey Henderson. Choices (B) and (C) only vary by one word, so be careful when making your choice.

10. **The correct answer is (A).** In all, the New York Yankees have won a record 26 World Series championships. They won in: 1923, 1927, 1928, 1932, 1936, 1937, 1938, 1939, 1941, 1943, 1947, 1949, 1950, 1951, 1952, 1953, 1956, 1958, 1961, 1962, 1977, 1978, 1996, 1998, 1999, and 2000.

11. **The correct answer is (D).** "The fix was in" during the 1919 World Series and the defeated Chicago White Sox became known as the "Black Sox."

12. **The correct answer is (C).** You may have been thrown off by choice (A), Canton, which is the location of the Football Hall of Fame, but the Baseball Hall of Fame is located in Cooperstown, New York.

13. **The correct answer is (B).** In 1995, Cal Ripken Jr. played in his 2,131st consecutive game, breaking Lou Gehrig's record of 2,130 consecutive games. This record is known as the "Iron Man" record.

14. **The correct answer is (D).** On July 24, 1983, George Brett's home run was ruled an out because it was decided by the umpires that there was too much pine tar on his bat. The Royals protested this ruling, and the game was completed in August of that year.

15. **The correct answer is (B).** In 1990, Bobby Thigpen saved a record 57 games for the Chicago White Sox.

16. **The correct answer is (C).** Eddie Matthews played for the Braves in Milwaukee, Boston, and Atlanta.

17. **The correct answer is (D).** In 1941, Joe DiMaggio hit safely in 56 consecutive games and collected a whopping 91 hits during the streak.

18. **The correct answer is (A).** *A League of Their Own* was a 1992 movie about a women's professional baseball league during World War II. *The Rookie* is a baseball movie, and choice (C), *There's No Crying in*

Baseball, refers to a famous line in the movie *A League of Their Own* said by Tom Hanks. Choice (D) mentions *The Georgia Peaches,* which was the name of one of the teams in *A League of Their Own.*

19. **The correct answer is (C).** Currently, Major League Baseball plays 162 games in a season, the most games per season of any professional sport. If you didn't know the answer, but you are familiar with baseball, you can probably eliminate choices (A) and (B) as having too few games. So, you once again can narrow your choices down to two and have a 50 percent chance of getting the question correct.

20. **The correct answer is (C).** The battery is defined as the pitcher and the catcher.

21. **The correct answer is (A).** Ty Cobb retired holding nearly all of the offensive records in baseball. Many of his records have since fallen, but the record for highest career batting average still belongs to Cobb.

22. **The correct answer is (C).** This question asks "which *pitching duo* of brothers," so you can eliminate choice (B)—Joe and Dom DiMaggio were brothers, but they were both outfielders, not pitchers. The brothers in choice (A), Jim and Gaylord Perry, held the record for most career wins with 529 until the record was broken by Joe and Phil Niekro, choice (C), with 539 combined career wins. Alan and Andy Benes, choice (D), are brothers, but they hold no record.

23. **The correct answer is (B).** Hank Aaron hit into an awful 328 double plays during his career. Reggie Jackson holds the record for the most career strikeouts (choice (A)) with 2,547. Choices (C) and (D) can be eliminated if you know Hank Aaron is the Home Run King, because it's a safe bet that if he holds a career home run record, he probably does not hold a record that has to do with missing the most games.

24. **The correct answer is (B).** To win baseball's Triple Crown in hitting, a player must lead the league in batting average, home runs, and RBIs. These are arguably the three most important offensive categories.

25. **The correct answer is (D).** To win baseball's Triple Crown in pitching, a player must lead the league in wins, strikeouts, and ERA (earned-run average).

26. **The correct answer is (B).** Fred Lynn hit a grand slam off Atlee Hammaker to become the first and only player to hit a grand slam in an All-Star game.

27. **The correct answer is (A).** Stengel and McGraw both won an incredible ten championships during their managerial careers.

28. **The correct answer is (D).** The pitcher's mound in Major League Baseball must be 60'6" from home plate.

29. **The correct answer is (B).** In the very first game of Yankee Stadium's inaugural season, Babe Ruth hit a home run.

30. **The correct answer is (C).** Cubs slugger Hack Wilson drove in 191 RBIs in 1930, setting both the National League and Major League record for RBIs in a season.

31. **The correct answer is (D).** In 1988, Orel Hershiser pitched 59 consecutive innings without giving up an earned run.

32. **The correct answer is (D).** There is no rule about a hit base runner that charges the pitcher with a balk. This is a negative question, so you are looking for the answer that is *not* true. Choices (A) through (C) are all true of a balk, so choice (D) is correct.

33. **The correct answer is (B).** Robinson played for the Brooklyn Dodgers during his historic season in 1947. This is an important fact in not only baseball history, but American history, so if you didn't know this before you took this test, remember it!

34. **The correct answer is (D).** The Houston Astros paid Nolan Ryan a $1,000,000 salary in 1979, making him the first major league baseball player to reach that salary plateau.

35. **The correct answer is (D).** All of the choices are expansion teams. The Devil Rays and Diamondbacks both became official major league teams in 1998. The Rockies and Marlins entered the league in 1993.

36. **The correct answer is (C).** Even though Mario Mendoza had a career batting average of .215, a player is said to be below the Mendoza Line if he bats below .200. The rest of the answer choices seem kind of silly, and although one might say those things about a poor hitter, choice (C) should seem most appropriate in the context of this test.

37. **The correct answer is (D).** Chan Ho Park became the first Korean-born player to ever play in the majors when he debuted with the Dodgers in 1994.

38. **The correct answer is (B).** On May 10, 1967, Hank Aaron hit the only inside-the-park home run of his career. If you know that inside-the-park home runs are pretty rare, you can eliminate choices (C) and (D) as too many, which leaves you with 0 or 1. Since the question was being asked in the first place, you can assume that he hit at least one, so select choice (B).

39. **The correct answer is (C).** In the last line of Ernest Lawrence Thayer's classic poem "Casey at the Bat," the "mighty Casey" strikes out and the author says "there is no joy in Mudville."

40. **The correct answer is (A).** There are more than two times as many pitchers in the Hall of Fame as there are players from any other position.

41. **The correct answer is (C).** Carl Yastrzemski won the Triple Crown in 1967 with 121 RBIs, 44 homers and a .326 average.

42. **The correct answer is (A).** Many people forget that Babe Ruth was actually a pitcher and a pretty good one. In 1916, Babe Ruth actually pitched 14 innings in a single World Series game.

43. **The correct answer is (D).** Hank Aaron, Stan Musial, and Willie Mays each played in an amazing 24 All-Star games.

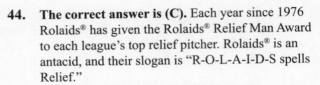

44. **The correct answer is (C).** Each year since 1976 Rolaids® has given the Rolaids® Relief Man Award to each league's top relief pitcher. Rolaids® is an antacid, and their slogan is "R-O-L-A-I-D-S spells Relief."

45. **The correct answer is (B).** Ryan and Damon Minor each played in the majors in 2002. All of the other choices are sets of twins, but none are currently active in the major leagues.

46. **The correct answer is (D).** Shortstops have recorded 6 of the 11 unassisted triple plays in major league history.

47. **The correct answer is (D).** Tim Stoddard's final-at-bat home run was also the first of his career.

48. **The correct answer is (B).** In 1938, Johnny Vander Meer pitched a no-hitter on June 11 and then another on June 15.

49. **The correct answer is (D).** In 1912, Ty Cobb stole home an amazing 8 times and he went on to steal home 54 times in his career.

50. **The correct answer is (A).** The Giants can claim 23 of the more than 250 members of the Hall of Fame, a relatively large percentage of the membership considering the number of teams that exist today and the number of teams that have come and gone over the years.

51. **The correct answer is (D).** There was one on base and Ralph Branca didn't want to risk putting another on for Willie Mays, so he had no choice but to pitch to Bobby Thomson. On the second pitch to him, Thomson hit it over the left-field fence for the game-winning home run.

52. **The correct answer is (B).** With a 392-foot shot into the left-field bleachers at SBC Park on September 17, 2004, Barry Bonds became the third player, after Hank Aaron and Babe Ruth, to hit 700 home runs in his career.

CHAPTER 2

Goal Line Stand:
Football

53. The championship game of the National Football League (NFL) is which of the following?

    (A) The World Series of Football

    (B) The World Cup

    (C) The Super Bowl

    (D) The Sugar Bowl

54. Who is the all-time leading rusher in the NFL?

    (A) Barry Sanders

    (B) Walter Payton

    (C) Emmitt Smith

    (D) Jim Brown

> If winning isn't everything, why do they keep score?
> —VINCE LOMBARDI

55. Which award is given annually to college football's best player?

(A) Lombardi Award

(B) Heisman Trophy

(C) Thorpe Award

(D) Outland Trophy

56. Which of the following penalties results in an automatic first down?

(A) Offside

(B) Delay of game

(C) Neutral zone infraction

(D) Defensive pass interference

57. Which two teams were involved the famous "Ice Bowl"?

(A) Packers and Cowboys

(B) Dolphins and Raiders

(C) Bills and Bears

(D) Packers and Bears

58. Former Atlanta Falcons coach Jerry Glanville was famous for leaving tickets for whom at each of the Falcons' home games?

(A) His mother

(B) The Pope

(C) The President

(D) Elvis

59. Which college football team has won the most national championships?

(A) Alabama

(B) Notre Dame

(C) Ohio State

(D) Oklahoma State

60. Which of the following teams was the only NFL team to ever record a perfect season?

  (A) Miami Dolphins, 1972

  (B) Chicago Bears, 1985

  (C) Baltimore Colts, 1969

  (D) Washington Redskins, 1964

61. Which of the following quarterbacks threw the pass that resulted in the "Immaculate Reception"?

  (A) John Elway

  (B) Joe Namath

  (C) Joe Montana

  (D) Terry Bradshaw

62. Who holds the record for the most career points in the NFL?

  (A) Jerry Rice

  (B) George Blanda

  (C) Gary Anderson

  (D) Dan Marino

63. Who holds the dubious NFL record for most career fumbles?

  (A) Warren Moon

  (B) Kerry Collins

  (C) Ickey Woods

  (D) Jack Kemp

64. Who holds the NCAA record for most yards rushing in a single game?'

  (A) O. J. Simpson

  (B) Barry Sanders

  (C) LaDainian Tomlinson

  (D) Thurman Thomas

65. Which of the following players once recorded more than 2,000 receiving yards in a single NFL season?

(A) Andre Reed

(B) Steve Largent

(C) Jerry Rice

(D) None of the above

66. Who holds the record for wins as an NCAA (all divisions) football coach?

(A) Bear Bryant

(B) Joe Paterno

(C) Bobby Bowden

(D) Eddie Robinson

67. Which NFL team lost a shameful 26 consecutive games in 1976 and 1977?

(A) Tampa Bay Buccaneers

(B) New Orleans Saints

(C) Cincinnati Bengals

(D) Cleveland Browns

68. Which of the following records does Dan Marino *not* hold?

(A) Most career touchdowns

(B) Most passing yards in a single game

(C) Most touchdowns in a single season

(D) Most passing yards in a single season

69. Who holds the NCAA (all divisions) record for most total yards in a season?

(A) Andre Ware

(B) David Klingler

(C) Steve McNair

(D) David Carr

70. Which of the following numbers is the NFL record for sacks in a single game, a record owned by the late Derrick Thomas?

    (A) 7

    (B) 9.5

    (C) 12

    (D) 12.5

71. Which 1985 NFL team recorded a record and a video called "The Super Bowl Shuffle"?

    (A) New England Patriots

    (B) Denver Broncos

    (C) Washington Redskins

    (D) Chicago Bears

72. The newest NFL team is which of the following?

    (A) Houston Texans

    (B) Tennessee Titans

    (C) Baltimore Ravens

    (D) Colorado Avalanche

73. Which USFL team won the first USFL championship game?

    (A) New Jersey Generals

    (B) Michigan Panthers

    (C) Philadelphia Stars

    (D) Jacksonville Bulls

74. Which school currently has the most former players who have been inducted into the Pro Football Hall of Fame?

    (A) Alabama

    (B) Notre Dame

    (C) Ohio State

    (D) USC

75. LSU's Tiger Stadium is often referred to by which of the following nicknames?

(A) "The Jungle"

(B) "The Swamp"

(C) "Death Valley"

(D) "The Cage"

76. In 1966, Washington set an NFL record for scoring in a game by posting how many points?

(A) 60

(B) 66

(C) 70

(D) 72

77. George Blanda holds which two NFL records for longevity?

(A) Most seasons played and most games played

(B) Most seasons played and most games played for the same team

(C) Most consecutive seasons and most consecutive games played

(D) Most games played and most seasons played with different teams

78. Which of the following coaches coached in both the Super Bowl and the Grey Cup of the Canadian Football League?

(A) Jim Mora

(B) Marv Levy

(C) Paul Brown

(D) Vince Lombardi

79. What is the nickname for the annual grudge match between the football teams of Alabama and Auburn?

(A) The "Egg Bowl"

(B) The "Toilet Bowl"

(C) The "Iron Bowl"

(D) The "Sugar Bowl"

80. What is a football official signaling if he has his palms together above his head?

(A) Touchback

(B) TV time out

(C) Safety

(D) Roughing the passer

81. What was the nickname of former Chicago Bear William Perry?

(A) "The Grizzly"

(B) "The Microwave"

(C) "The Deep Freeze"

(D) "The Refrigerator"

82. Don Shula and Tom Landry each coached in how many playoff games during their NFL careers?

(A) 15

(B) 21

(C) 26

(D) 36

83. What NFL legend was drafted in the first round of the 1985 USFL draft by the Birmingham Stallions?

(A) Jerry Rice

(B) Steve Young

(C) Jim Kelly

(D) Mike Rozier

84. Who was the only college football player to win the Heisman Trophy twice?

(A) Earl Campbell

(B) Archie Griffin

(C) O. J. Simpson

(D) Jay Berwanger

85. Which defensive menace not only holds the record for interceptions in a season (14) but also set the record as a rookie?

(A) Deion Sanders

(B) Darrell Green

(C) Dick "Night Train" Lane

(D) Ronnie Lott

86. Which college football team plays in the stadium with the largest seating capacity?

(A) Purdue

(B) Notre Dame

(C) Tennessee

(D) Michigan

87. How many yards was the longest field goal ever kicked in NFL history?

(A) 51 yards

(B) 55 yards

(C) 63 yards

(D) 69 yards

88. What is the largest conference in the NCAA?

(A) The Big Ten

(B) The Big 12

(C) The SEC

(D) The MAC

89. Who holds the record for the longest run from scrimmage on Monday Night Football?

  (A) Earl Campbell

  (B) Tony Dorsett

  (C) Bo Jackson

  (D) Marcus Allen

90. Who holds the NFL record for most touchdowns in a season with 26?

  (A) Emmitt Smith

  (B) John Riggins

  (C) Marshall Faulk

  (D) Jerry Rice

91. Which of the following NFL teams with animal mascots does *not* depict an animal on the team's helmets?

  (A) Falcons

  (B) Dolphins

  (C) Panthers

  (D) Rams

92. Which of the following is the only player to score 200 touchdowns in his career?

  (A) Don Hutson

  (B) Red Grange

  (C) Art Monk

  (D) Jerry Rice

93. What is the NFL record number of field goals made in a game by one player?

  (A) 7

  (B) 8

  (C) 9

  (D) 10

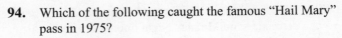

94. Which of the following caught the famous "Hail Mary" pass in 1975?

(A) Franco Harris

(B) John Stallworth

(C) Ahmad Rashaad

(D) Drew Pearson

95. Former Green Bay Packer Max McGee has the distinction of accomplishing which of the following firsts?

(A) First touchdown in Packer history

(B) First touchdown at Lambeau Field

(C) First Super Bowl touchdown

(D) First player to throw and catch a touchdown in the same game

96. Which former Heisman winner went to Canada and led his teams to three Grey Cup championships?

(A) Warren Moon

(B) Doug Flutie

(C) Rob Johnson

(D) Andre Ware

97. The Yale-Harvard game of 1968 is legendary for which of the following reasons?

(A) Nobody attended the game.

(B) The game was played in an airplane hangar.

(C) The game was hard fought and ended in a 29–29 tie.

(D) The game ended in a 0–0 tie.

98. Which of the following players once gained 262 yards in a single quarter and 402 yards total against a Michigan team that had only allowed four touchdowns in the previous two seasons?

(A) "Crazy Legs" Hirsch

(B) Red Grange

(C) Larry Csonka

(D) Johnny Unitas

99. Which NFL quarterback legend holds the dubious record of most interceptions?

(A) George Blanda

(B) Johnny Unitas

(C) Joe Montana

(D) Joe Namath

100. Washington Redskin Timmie Smith accomplished which of the following amazing feats during Super Bowl XXII?

(A) Scored a touchdown in five different ways

(B) Scored five touchdowns

(C) Ran for 204 yards despite rushing for only 126 yards all season

(D) Intercepted five consecutive passes

101. The Little Brown Jug is the trophy awarded to the winner of which of the following college rivalries?

(A) Ole Miss vs. Mississippi State

(B) Texas vs. Texas A&M

(C) Miami vs. Florida State

(D) Michigan vs. Minnesota

102. What was the worst defeat ever recorded in college football?

(A) 75–2

(B) 111–13

(C) 127–0

(D) 222–0

103. What ABC *Monday Night Football* announcer was known as "The Mouth"?

(A) Al Michaels

(B) Howard Cosell

(C) John Madden

(D) Dennis Miller

CHAPTER 2 ANSWERS

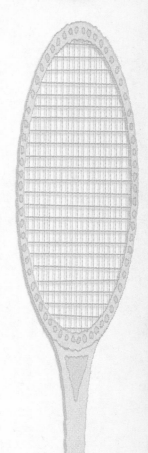

53. **The correct answer is (C).** The Super Bowl is played annually between the National Football Conference champion and the American Football Conference champion. Choice (B), World Cup is a soccer trophy (football, to non-Americans) and choice (D), Sugar Bowl, is a college football championship game.

54. **The correct answer is (C).** In the 2002 season, Emmitt Smith passed Walter Payton and moved into sole possession of first place on the all-time rushing list.

55. **The correct answer is (B).** Each year, New York's Downtown Athletic Club presents the nation's best collegiate player with the Heisman Trophy.

56. **The correct answer is (D).** Defensive pass interference results in an automatic first down for the offensive team regardless of where the foul occurred. All of the other choices are also penalties, but none of them results in an automatic first down.

57. **The correct answer is (A).** The Packers and Cowboys played the famous "Ice Bowl" on December 31, 1967, in the NFL title game.

58. **The correct answer is (D).** Although the tickets were never picked up, Jerry Glanville left Falcons tickets for Elvis before every home game during his tenure as coach in Atlanta.

59. **The correct answer is (B).** Notre Dame has won nine national championships since national championships officially began in 1936.

60. **The correct answer is (A).** The 1972 Miami Dolphins went 16–0, a feat never matched before or since in the NFL.

61. **The correct answer is (D).** In 1972, Terry Bradshaw threw a pass against the Raiders intended for "Frenchy" Fuqua. Somehow, the pass was deflected backward 15 yards and was caught by Franco Harris who ran for a touchdown for the Steelers.

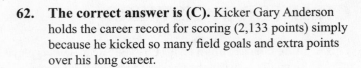

62. **The correct answer is (C).** Kicker Gary Anderson holds the career record for scoring (2,133 points) simply because he kicked so many field goals and extra points over his long career.

63. **The correct answer is (A).** Warren Moon fumbled the football an incredible 161 times during his NFL career.

64. **The correct answer is (C).** O. J. Simpson, Barry Sanders, and Thurman Thomas were all great rushers in college and went on to have great careers in the NFL. LaDainian Tomlinson is at the beginning of his NFL career, so he's not a legend yet like the other choices, but in 1999, he rushed for 406 yards against UTEP, setting the NCAA record for most rushing yards in a single game.

65. **The correct answer is (D).** No player in NFL history has ever recorded more than 2,000 receiving yards in a single season.

66. **The correct answer is (D).** Eddie Robinson won an amazing 408 games during his career at Grambling. Bear Bryant has 323 wins, Joe Paterno has won 343 games so far in his career (all with Penn State), and Bobby Bowden has won 351 games so far in his career.

67. **The correct answer is (A).** Over two woeful seasons, the Tampa Bay Bucs lost 26 consecutive games, seven more than the next team in the league, which had 19 consecutive losses.

68. **The correct answer is (B).** Norm Van Brocklin passed for 554 yards in a single game in 1951. This was a negative question, so you needed to look for the answer that was *not* true. Did you circle the word *not* in the question so you would remember that it was a negative question?

69. **The correct answer is (C).** Steve McNair amassed 5,799 yards of total offense in 1994, placing him first on the all-time list.

70. **The correct answer is (A).** In a single game, Derrick Thomas recorded 7 sacks, more than many players record in a single season.

71. **The correct answer is (D).** The 1985 Chicago Bears recorded "The Super Bowl Shuffle" and then went on to win the Super Bowl.

72. **The correct answer is (A).** The Houston Texans took the field for the first time in the 2002 season. If you didn't know the answer, you were hopefully able to at least eliminate choice (D), since the Colorado Avalanche is a hockey team, and give yourself a better chance at guessing.

73. **The correct answer is (B).** The Michigan Panthers won the first USFL championship in 1983.

74. **The correct answer is (B).** All of the schools listed in the choices have graduated football hall of fame players, but the one with the most players in the Pro Football Hall of Fame is Notre Dame.

75. **The correct answer is (C).** Recognized as one of the toughest places to play in college football, Tiger Stadium is often called "Death Valley."

76. **The correct answer is (D).** The Redskins scored a record 72 points against the New York Giants in 1966.

77. **The correct answer is (A).** George Blanda played in 26 different seasons and in 340 games, both NFL records.

78. **The correct answer is (B).** Marv Levy coached Buffalo in the Super Bowl and Montreal in the Grey Cup. He won the Grey Cup twice, but went 0–4 in the Super Bowl.

79. **The correct answer is (C).** The bitter rivalry between Alabama and Auburn reaches a climax every year in the Iron Bowl. Choices (A) and (B) are pretty silly, so you can eliminate them. You are then left with choice (C), the Iron Bowl, and choice (D), the Sugar Bowl. The Sugar Bowl is part of the Bowl Championship Series in the NCAA, and the teams that play in it are different every year, so that choice can be eliminated since the question says *annually*. This leaves you with choice (C), the correct answer.

80. **The correct answer is (C).** Raising one's hands above the head with palms together is the official signal for a safety.

81. **The correct answer is (D).** Because of his enormous size, William Perry was known as "the Refrigerator" or "the Fridge."

82. **The correct answer is (D).** Shula, with the Colts and Dolphins, and Landry, with the Cowboys, each coached in 36 post-season games. This may seem like a high number, but remember that both are legendary coaches.

83. **The correct answer is (A).** If you are a casual fan, you may have been tempted to pick choice (E), Mike Rozier, since his name is not as well known as the other choices and the question mentions the USFL. But Jerry Rice was actually drafted by the Birmingham Stallions of the USFL; however, he chose to sign with the 49ers, the NFL team that also drafted him.

84. **The correct answer is (B).** As a junior at Ohio State University, Archie Griffin was named to every All-American team and was called "the greatest football player I've ever coached" by Woody Hayes. He smashed the all-time record for running backs in the Big Ten, amassing 4,064 yards. As a senior, he extended his overall yardage to 5,175.

85. **The correct answer is (C).** In 1952, his rookie season, Dick "Night Train" Lane caught 14 interceptions, a record that still stands.

86. **The correct answer is (D).** Michigan's stadium holds a whopping 107,501 people. Tennessee's stadium is the next largest (and formerly the largest), seating 106,538 people. Notre Dame's stadium holds 80,000 people. Purdue's stadium held 67,332 people in 2002, but renovations in 2003 dropped seating capacity to 62,500.

87. **The correct answer is (C).** Tom Dempsey of New Orleans and Jason Elam of Denver each kicked a 63-yard field goal. Dempsey's came in 1970 and Elam's came in 1998.

88. **The correct answer is (D).** The MAC, or Mid-Atlantic Conference, actually has 13 teams, which makes it the largest conference in the NCAA.

89. **The correct answer is (B).** Tony Dorsett ran for a 99-yard touchdown on Monday Night Football on January 3, 1983.

90. **The correct answer is (C).** Marshall Faulk scored 26 touchdowns in 2000 with the St. Louis Rams.

91. **The correct answer is (D).** The Rams have ram horns on their helmets but no rams. The Falcons have a falcon, the Dolphins have a dolphin, and the Panthers have a panther on their helmets.

92. **The correct answer is (D).** Jerry Rice scored his 200th career touchdown on Monday Night Football on November 11, 2002.

93. **The correct answer is (A).** Three different players have kicked seven field goals in a game, the latest being Chris Boniol for the Cowboys in 1996.

94. **The correct answer is (D).** Drew Pearson caught the pass for the Cowboys against the Vikings in 1975. You'll remember from a previous question that Franco Harris was involved in the "Immaculate Reception."

95. **The correct answer is (C).** Max McGee scored the first Super Bowl touchdown in 1967 for the Green Bay Packers.

96. **The correct answer is (B).** After five seasons of being knocked around in the NFL, Doug Flutie went to the CFL where he won the MVP award six times and won the Grey Cup three times. He then returned to the NFL with the Buffalo Bills and more recently with the San Diego Chargers.

97. **The correct answer is (C).** Harvard came from behind to tie the game at 29 with a two-point conversion that gave Harvard a share of the Ivy League championship. Eliminate choices (A) and (B) as both being really unlikely, you're left with a choice of two

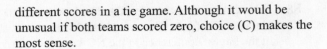

different scores in a tie game. Although it would be unusual if both teams scored zero, choice (C) makes the most sense.

98. **The correct answer is (B).** Red Grange ran for five touchdowns and threw for another against Michigan in 1924, in what is considered to be one of the greatest games in college football history.

99. **The correct answer is (A).** George Blanda threw 277 interceptions in his career, nine more than John Hadl, who holds second place.

100. **The correct answer is (C).** Timmie Smith rushed for 126 yards during the season prior to Super Bowl XXII and then rushed for just over 600 yards in the next two seasons; however, during Super Bowl XXII, Smith became the only person to ever rush for 200 yards in the Super Bowl.

101. **The correct answer is (D).** The Little Brown Jug was first awarded in 1909 to the winner of the Michigan-Minnesota game.

102. **The correct answer is (D).** Georgia Tech pounded Cumberland 222–0 in 1916 in a blowout the likes of which the football world may never see again.

103. **The correct answer is (B).** Howard Cosell began covering sports for ABC in 1956 and was identified especially with *Monday Night Football* (1970–84). As a vocal advocate for Muhammad Ali, Cosell's often abrasive style earned him the nickname "The Mouth."

CHAPTER 3

Drive to the Hoop:
Basketball

104. The person most often credited with the invention of basketball is which of the following?

(A) James Springfield

(B) James Canton

(C) James Naismith

(D) James Cooper

105. Which of the following teams won 11 NBA championships between 1957 and 1969?

(A) Lakers

(B) Celtics

(C) Warriors

(D) 76ers

> I can accept failure, but I can't accept not trying.
> —MICHAEL JORDAN

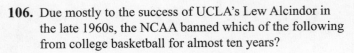

106. Due mostly to the success of UCLA's Lew Alcindor in the late 1960s, the NCAA banned which of the following from college basketball for almost ten years?

(A) The blocked shot

(B) The three-point shot

(C) The behind-the-back-pass

(D) The dunk

107. Who holds the NCAA single season scoring average record with 44.5 points per game?

(A) Michael Jordan

(B) Pete Maravich

(C) Allen Iverson

(D) Larry Bird

108. Lisa Leslie of the Los Angeles Sparks became the first player to do which of the following in a WNBA game?

(A) Record a triple double

(B) Dunk

(C) Foul out

(D) Score a field goal

109. Who holds the NBA career record for most assists to the same person?

(A) John Havlicek

(B) Magic Johnson

(C) Gary Payton

(D) John Stockton

110. Who is the only player to have 200 steals and 100 blocked shots in a single NBA season?

(A) Wilt Chamberlain

(B) Bill Russell

(C) Michael Jordan

(D) Gary Payton

111. Which accomplishment can the women's basketball teams at the University of Texas, the University of Tennessee, and University of Connecticut all claim?

  (A) More than fifty alumnae from each school in the WNBA

  (B) Eight national championships each

  (C) An undefeated championship season

  (D) Defeating an NCAA men's team during the regular season

112. Who once scored 100 points in an NBA game?

  (A) Wilt Chamberlain

  (B) Pete Maravich

  (C) David Robinson

  (D) Michael Jordan

113. What player won All-Star Game MVP, NBA MVP, and NBA Finals MVP awards in 2000?

  (A) Michael Jordan

  (B) Kobe Bryant

  (C) Shaquille O'Neal

  (D) Tim Duncan

114. Which of the following is the all-time winningest NCAA Division I men's basketball program in terms of both wins and winning percentage?

  (A) Kentucky

  (B) Duke

  (C) Kansas

  (D) UCLA

115. Who is the shortest person to have ever played in the NBA?

  (A) Spud Webb

  (B) Muggsy Bogues

  (C) Nate "Tiny" Archibald

  (D) Louis Klotz

116. Who scored the first three-point basket in NBA history?

    (A)   Wes Unseld

    (B)   Gene Stump

    (C)   Chris Ford

    (D)   Larry Bird

117. What team won the very first NBA game?

    (A)   Philadelphia Warriors

    (B)   New York Knicks

    (C)   Toronto Huskies

    (D)   Chicago Stags

118. Lynette Woodard became the first woman to ever do which of the following?

    (A)   Dunk in an NCAA game

    (B)   Coach a WNBA team

    (C)   Play in the NBA

    (D)   Play for the Harlem Globetrotters

119. Which of the following teams recorded the best regular season record in NBA history?

    (A)   Chicago Bulls

    (B)   Boston Celtics

    (C)   Los Angeles Lakers

    (D)   Philadelphia 76ers

120. Who holds the record for youngest player drafted in NBA history?

    (A)   Jermaine O'Neal

    (B)   Martell Webster

    (C)   Andrew Bynum

    (D)   Kobe Bryant

121. Which of the following players was drafted by the NBA out of the U.S. Naval Academy then served two years with the Navy before joining his team in the NBA?

   (A) Jerry Lucas

   (B) David Robinson

   (C) Tim Duncan

   (D) Bill Walton

122. Which of the following was called "the Dream Team?"

   (A) The 1995–96 Chicago Bulls

   (B) The 1992 U.S. Olympic Team

   (C) The 1979–80 Los Angeles Lakers

   (D) The 1989–90 Duke Blue Devils

123. What was the nickname of the Houston Cougars during the years that Clyde Drexler and Akeem Olajuwon played there?

   (A) "High-Flying Houston"

   (B) "The Dream Gliders"

   (C) "Phi Slamma Jamma"

   (D) "Bad Mamma Jamma"

124. Who was the first MVP of the WNBA?

   (A) Lisa Leslie

   (B) Pat Summitt

   (C) Sue Bird

   (D) Cynthia Cooper

125. Who is the only woman to score 100 or more points in a college basketball game?

   (A) Cheryl Miller

   (B) Chamique Holdsclaw

   (C) Jackie Stiles

   (D) None of the above

126. What word was used to describe a famous and amazing move by Michael Jordan in the 1991 NBA Finals as he moved the ball from one hand to another in mid-air and scored a layup?

(A) "Amazing"

(B) "Spectacular"

(C) "Un-be-lievable"

(D) "Glorious"

127. Of all the NBA teams to win the NBA championship between 1986 and 2002, which of the following is the only team that did not win at least two consecutive championships?

(A) Houston Rockets

(B) Detroit Pistons

(C) San Antonio Spurs

(D) Chicago Bulls

128. Which of the following is a difference between men's and women's basketball?

(A) The length of the court

(B) The height of the rim

(C) The width of the court

(D) The size of the ball

129. James Naismith, according to tradition, used what as the very first basket in his new game called basketball?

(A) Garbage can

(B) Peach basket

(C) Cardboard box

(D) Wooden crate

130. Before Magic Johnson and Larry Bird battled in the NBA, they battled in the 1979 NCAA finals for which two teams, respectively?

(A) Michigan State and Indiana State

(B) Michigan and Indiana

(C) Michigan State and Indiana

(D) Michigan and Indiana State

131. Who is the only coach to win championship titles in the ABL, the ABA, and the NBA?

(A) Cotton Fitzsimmons

(B) Chuck Daly

(C) Red Auerbach

(D) Bill Sharman

132. Which of the following players, known for his finger rolls, went by the nickname "Iceman"?

(A) Elvin Hayes

(B) Walt Frazier

(C) George Gervin

(D) Bill Laimbeer

133. Which of the following players is listed in the NBA's 50 greatest players and pitched for the Chicago White Sox in 1962 and 1963?

(A) Dave Cowens

(B) Dave Bing

(C) Dave DeBusschere

(D) Dolph Schayes

134. Which of the following players is the NBA's all-time leading scorer with 38,387 career points?

(A) Kareem Abdul-Jabbar

(B) Karl Malone

(C) Michael Jordan

(D) Wilt Chamberlain

135. Which of the following is the NBA's all-time highest career free-throw percentage owned by Mark Price?

(A) .804 FT%

(B) .888 FT%

(C) .904 FT%

(D) .999 FT%

136. Which men's basketball team was the winningest NCAA team in both the 1960s and 1970s?

(A) Kentucky

(B) North Carolina

(C) Duke

(D) UCLA

137. Which of the following players owns the NCAA Division I record for most points scored in a season?

(A) Jackie Stiles

(B) Cheryl Miller

(C) Sheryl Swoopes

(D) Cindy Brown

138. "The Pearl" was the nickname for which NBA legend?

(A) Pete Maravich

(B) Earl Monroe

(C) Patrick Ewing

(D) Scottie Pippen

139. Which player never played for the Lakers?

(A) James Worthy

(B) Jerry West

(C) Elgin Baylor

(D) Nate Thurmond

140. Who are the only two players to lead the NCAA in scoring for three seasons?

(A) Oscar Robertson and Allan Houston

(B) Allan Houston and Pete Maravich

(C) Pete Maravich and Oscar Robertson

(D) Shaquille O'Neal and Allen Iverson

141. Which NBA legend holds the record for most rebounds in a career and the highest rebounds per game average?

(A) Bill Russell

(B) Dennis Rodman

(C) Bob Pettit

(D) Wilt Chamberlain

142. Who holds the NBA record for most career steals?

(A) Gary Payton

(B) Michael Jordan

(C) John Stockton

(D) Bob Cousey

143. Which of the following players holds the NCAA Division I record for most career blocked shots?

(A) David Robinson

(B) Tim Duncan

(C) Adonal Foyle

(D) Alonzo Mourning

144. Which NCAA team holds the record for the longest winning streak at 88 games?

(A) Temple

(B) Arizona

(C) Duke

(D) UCLA

145. Who is the only college coach to lead four different teams to the NCAA tournament?

(A) Eddie Sutton

(B) John Thompson

(C) Rick Pitino

(D) John Wooden

146. Who was the head coach of the first U.S. women's Olympic basketball team to win a gold medal?

(A) Leon Barmore

(B) Pat Summitt

(C) Tara Vanderveer

(D) Jody Conradt

147. Which NBA star won a season-long game of H-O-R-S-E among NBA stars in the 1970s?

(A) Oscar Robertson

(B) Bill Walton

(C) Paul Westphal

(D) Pete Maravich

148. What NBA legend is actually the silhouette used in the NBA logo?

(A) Jerry West

(B) John Havlicek

(C) Larry Bird

(D) Bob Cousey

149. What innovation was added to the game of basketball in the 1954–55 season that changed the game forever?

(A) The three-point line

(B) The 24 second shot clock

(C) The no-dunk rule

(D) The free-throw line

150. Who holds the NBA record for points per game with 31.0?

(A) Wilt Chamberlain

(B) Allen Iverson

(C) Shaquille O'Neal

(D) Michael Jordan

151. The AP Player of the Year in women's college basketball from 1995 to 2000 came from one of which two schools in each of those years?

(A) Stanford and UConn

(B) UConn and Texas

(C) Texas and Tennessee

(D) UConn and Tennessee

152. Which NBA player was voted as a starter for the All-Star Game even though he had retired and then went on to win the MVP award for the game?

(A) Larry Bird

(B) Isiah Thomas

(C) Magic Johnson

(D) Bill Walton

153. Over whom did Michael Jordan hit "The Shot" in 1989 to knock Cleveland out of the playoffs?

(A) Mark Price

(B) Brad Daugherty

(C) Craig Ehlo

(D) None of the above

154. Who was the first Chinese player to play in an NBA game?

(A) Hai Rui

(B) Wang Zhizhi

(C) Hu Weidong

(D) Yao Ming

CHAPTER 3 ANSWERS

104. **The correct answer is (C).** James Naismith is credited with the invention of basketball in 1891.

105. **The correct answer is (B).** Led by Bill Russell, the Boston Celtics maintained a dynasty for thirteen years and won 11 NBA championships between 1957 and 1969.

106. **The correct answer is (D).** The NCAA actually banned the dunk until 1978 because of Lew Alcindor's dominance of the college game.

107. **The correct answer is (B).** Jordan, Iverson, and Bird were all great college players, but Pete Maravich holds the record with an average of 44.5 points per game at LSU during the 1970 season.

108. **The correct answer is (B).** In the 2002 season, Lisa Leslie became the first WNBA player to dunk in a game.

109. **The correct answer is (D).** John Stockton, who holds the NBA record for career assists, also holds the NBA record for assists in a career to the same person. The lucky beneficiary of those assists was Karl Malone.

110. **The correct answer is (C).** Michael Jordan is the only player to ever record 200 steals and 100 blocked shots in a single season, and he's done it twice.

111. **The correct answer is (C).** Each of the three schools has won a national championship at the end of an undefeated season. Choice (A) is not likely, and you can eliminate choice (D), since the men and women do not play each other during the regular season.

112. **The correct answer is (A).** In 1962, Wilt Chamberlain scored 100 points against the New York Knicks.

113. **The correct answer is (C).** In 2000, Shaquille O'Neal became just the third person to sweep MVP honors for the season, capturing the All-Star Game MVP, which he shared with San Antonio's Tim Duncan, NBA MVP, and NBA Finals MVP awards. O'Neal joined Willis Reed (1970) and Michael Jordan (1996).

114. **The correct answer is (A).** Kentucky, through 2001–02, has won 1795 games at a .763 clip.

115. **The correct answer is (B).** Standing at 5'3" tall, Muggsy Bogues is the shortest player to ever play in the NBA.

116. **The correct answer is (C).** On October 12, 1979, Chris Ford of the Boston Celtics scored the first three-point basket in NBA history with 3:48 left in the first quarter of a 114–106 victory over Houston. This game was also the first of Boston rookie Larry Bird.

117. **The correct answer is (B).** The New York Knicks defeated the Toronto Huskies 68–66 in the very first NBA game on November 1, 1946.

118. **The correct answer is (D).** Lynette Woodard, a four-time All-American (1978–81) from the University of Kansas, was the first female to play for the Harlem Globetrotters (1985–87). In 1992, Woodward became the first female to be enshrined in the GTE Academic All-American Hall of Fame. In 1997, she came out of retirement to play two seasons with the WNBA's Cleveland Rockers and the Detroit Shock.

119. **The correct answer is (A).** The Chicago Bulls posted a 72–10 record in the 1995–96 season on the way to another NBA championship.

120. **The correct answer is (C).** At 17 years, 8 months, and 2 days old, Andrew Bynum was drafted 10th in the first round of the 2005 draft by the Los Angeles Lakers.

121. **The correct answer is (B).** David Robinson finished school in 1987, and then began his rookie season with the San Antonio Spurs in 1989.

122. **The correct answer is (B).** The 1992 U.S. Olympic team led by the likes of Jordan, Bird, and Magic were known around the world as "the Dream Team."

123. **The correct answer is (C).** The Houston Cougars were considered a dunking fraternity of sorts, and they were given the name "Phi Slamma Jamma."

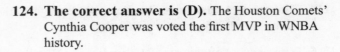

124. The correct answer is (D). The Houston Comets' Cynthia Cooper was voted the first MVP in WNBA history.

125. The correct answer is (D). No woman has broken the 100-point barrier in a college game.

126. The correct answer is (B). Marv Albert immortalized Jordan's move by declaring "a *spectacular* move by Michael Jordan."

127. The correct answer is (C). The San Antonio Spurs won a single NBA title in 1998–99. Hopefully, you were at least able to eliminate the Bulls right away, giving yourself a 1 in 3 chance of getting the answer correct.

128. The correct answer is (D). The size of a women's basketball is slightly smaller than a man's basketball.

129. The correct answer is (B). Naismith reportedly used a peach basket in the first game of basketball.

130. The correct answer is (A). Magic's Michigan State Spartans defeated Bird's Indiana State Sycamores in the 1979 NCAA championship game.

131. The correct answer is (D). Bill Sharman won championships with the ABL's Cleveland Pipers, the ABA's Utah Stars, and the NBA's Los Angeles Lakers.

132. The correct answer is (C). George "Iceman" Gervin was famous for his high-flying dunks and finger rolls during his NBA playing days.

133. The correct answer is (C). Dave DeBusschere, in addition to playing professional baseball, served as a player/coach in the NBA and became the league's youngest head coach ever at age 24.

134. The correct answer is (A). Kareem Abdul-Jabbar is the NBA's all-time leading scorer. Next on the list is Karl Malone with 35,378, followed by Wilt Chamberlain with 31,419, and Michael Jordan with 31,302.

135. The correct answer is (C). Price shot an unbelievable .904 from the free-throw line, just higher than Rick Barry's .900.

136. The correct answer is (D). UCLA led the NCAA in wins and winning percentage in the 1960s and the 1970s.

137. The correct answer is (A). Jackie Stiles scored 1,062 points, an NCAA record, for Southwest Missouri State in 2000–01.

138. The correct answer is (B). Earl "The Pearl" Monroe was a standout guard for the Bullets and the Knicks.

139. The correct answer is (D). Nate Thurmond played with San Francisco, Golden State, Chicago, and Cleveland but never with the Lakers.

140. The correct answer is (C). Two of the most prolific scorers in NCAA history, Maravich and Robertson, are the only players to lead the nation in scoring for three seasons.

141. The correct answer is (D). Wilt Chamberlain amassed more than 23,000 rebounds during his career and maintained an average of better than 22 rebounds per game.

142. The correct answer is (C). John Stockton holds not only the career assist record but also the career steals record.

143. The correct answer is (C). In only three years, Adonal Foyle set the NCAA record for blocked shots with 492.

144. The correct answer is (D). John Wooden coached UCLA to an amazing 88 game winning streak, a record that likely never will be broken.

145. The correct answer is (A). Eddie Sutton has taken Creighton, Arkansas, Kentucky, and Oklahoma State to "the dance," also known as the NCAA tournament.

146. The correct answer is (B). Tennessee Lady Vols head coach Pat Summitt led the U.S. Olympic team to a gold medal in 1984 in Los Angeles.

147. The correct answer is (C). Paul Westphal won the game of H-O-R-S-E, a game that was filled with trick shots and long range shots.

148. The correct answer is (A). The official logo of the NBA features a silhouette of Jerry West dribbling the basketball, which is why West is sometimes referred to as "the logo."

149. The correct answer is (B). In the 1954–55 season, because of the shot clock, the game of basketball was accelerated and was made more exciting because of the new, faster pace of the game.

150. The correct answer is (D). Michael Jordan currently holds the record for most points per game, 31.0, an average that is nearly a full point better than second place.

151. The correct answer is (D). From 1995 to 1997, the Player of the Year came from the University of Connecticut, and from 1998–2000 the Player of the Year came from Tennessee.

152. The correct answer is (C). Magic Johnson retired from the game in November 1991 and then won the All-Star MVP award in the 1992 game.

153. The correct answer is (C). Michael Jordan shot a perfect jumper over Craig Ehlo and then pumped his fist as Chicago knocked Cleveland out of the playoffs in 1989.

154. The correct answer is (B). On April 5, 2001, Wang Zhizhi of the Dallas Mavericks became the first Chinese player to compete in the NBA. Wang had six points and three rebounds in a 108–94 win over Atlanta.

CHAPTER 4

Off Its Moorings:
Hockey

155. What is a hat trick?

   (A) When a puck knocks a goalie's mask off

   (B) When every player on the team wears the same kind of helmet

   (C) When a player records three assists in a game

   (D) When a player scores three goals in a game

156. Traditionally, what is tossed onto the ice at Detroit Red Wings home games?

   (A) Hats

   (B) Roses

   (C) Buffalo wings

   (D) An octopus

> The game of hockey itself is very easy. It's the thinking about it that makes it hard.
> —CARL BREUER

157. Montreal, Toronto, Boston, Detroit, Chicago, and New York collectively are known as what?

(A) "The Original Six"

(B) "The Original Ice"

(C) "The Thin Ice"

(D) None of the above

158. The first NHL All-Star game was held as a benefit for what injured star?

(A) Eddie Shore

(B) Ace Bailey

(C) Howie Morenz

(D) Sylvio Mantha

159. What was the "Miracle on Ice"?

(A) The longest game in NHL history

(B) The U.S. victory over the USSR in the 1980 Olympics

(C) The game in which Wayne Gretzky became the all-time leading scorer

(D) Game 7 of the 2000 Stanley Cup Finals

160. How many different face-off spots are there on a modern hockey rink?

(A) 3

(B) 5

(C) 7

(D) 9

161. Who is the only member of an NHL team that cannot be a team captain?

(A) Goalie

(B) Forward

(C) Center

(D) Any member can be captain.

162. Which of the following awards is given to the league's most outstanding rookie each year in the NHL?

(A) The Hart Memorial Trophy

(B) The Bill Masterton Trophy

(C) The Conn Smythe Trophy

(D) The Calder Memorial Trophy

163. Who was the oldest player to ever play in an NHL All-Star Game?

(A) Wayne Gretzky

(B) Dit Clapper

(C) Bobby Orr

(D) Gordie Howe

164. Who was the first player to score 50 goals in a season?

(A) Bobby Orr

(B) Maurice Richard

(C) Armand Guidolin

(D) Mike Bossy

165. What is the other name for a hockey player's jersey?

(A) Jacket

(B) Coat

(C) Sweater

(D) Serape

166. In which season in the NHL was Andy Brown the last goalie to play without a mask?

(A) 1963–64

(B) 1973–74

(C) 1983–84

(D) 1993–94

167. Who is the top-scoring defenseman of all-time in the NHL?

(A)   Ray Bourque

(B)   Ted Lindsay

(C)   Eddie Shore

(D)   Paul Coffey

168. Who was known as "The Boss" and "The Goal Machine"?

(A)   Wayne Gretzky

(B)   Bobby Orr

(C)   Gordie Howe

(D)   Mike Bossy

169. The top college hockey player receives which of the following awards?

(A)   The Lady Byng Trophy

(B)   The Hobey Baker Award

(C)   The Calder Memorial Trophy

(D)   The Bill Masterton Trophy

170. The "Production Line" featuring Sid Abel, Ted Lindsay, and Gordie Howe was the mainstay of what NHL team?

(A)   New York Rangers

(B)   Boston Bruins

(C)   Detroit Red Wings

(D)   Chicago Blackhawks

171. Who is the oldest player to score 50 goals?

(A)   Gordie Howe

(B)   Jaromir Jagr

(C)   Marcel Dionne

(D)   Johnny Bucyk

172. What nickname did Sid Abel acquire after Maurice Richard broke his nose in a fight?

   (A) "Old Bootnose"

   (B) "Glass Face"

   (C) "Crooked Nose"

   (D) "Fragile Face"

173. What team was known for its famous "French Connection" line?

   (A) Detroit Red Wings

   (B) Montreal Canadiens

   (C) Edmonton Oilers

   (D) Buffalo Sabres

174. Who was the first great European player in the NHL?

   (A) Teemu Selanne

   (B) Borje Salming

   (C) Igor Larianov

   (D) Dominik Hasek

175. Who won the NHL's MVP award, the Hart Trophy, nine times in his first ten seasons?

   (A) Mario Lemieux

   (B) Wayne Gretzky

   (C) Bobby Orr

   (D) Gordie Howe

176. Who broke the legendary Mike Bossy's rookie goal scoring record?

   (A) Jaromir Jagr

   (B) Mario Lemieux

   (C) Teemu Selanne

   (D) Wayne Gretzky

177. Who holds the NHL record for career penalty minutes?

(A)   Ted Lindsay

(B)   Ray Bourque

(C)   Dave Williams

(D)   Eddie Shore

178. Bernie "Boom Boom" Geoffrion is credited for inventing which of the following?

(A)   The modern hockey jersey

(B)   The one-timer

(C)   The modern hockey mask

(D)   The slap shot

179. Which team has made the most Stanley Cup finals appearances?

(A)   Detroit Red Wings

(B)   Edmonton Oilers

(C)   Montreal Canadiens

(D)   New York Rangers

180. What has happened if a player has hit the puck "between the pipes"?

(A)   He has scored a goal.

(B)   He has scored an assist.

(C)   He has hit an opposing player's helmet with the puck.

(D)   He has hit an opposing player's midsection with the puck.

181. Who was the last player to play without a helmet?

(A)   Ken Morrow

(B)   Dave Williams

(C)   Ted Lindsay

(D)   Craig MacTavish

182. Who is the winningest coach in NHL history?

(A)   Al Arbour

(B)   Frank Boucher

(C)   Denis Potvin

(D)   Scotty Bowman

183. The Hockey Hall of Fame is located in which of the following cities?

(A)   Boston

(B)   Toronto

(C)   Montreal

(D)   New York

184. What is the record number of both goals and assists in a single game?

(A)   5

(B)   6

(C)   7

(D)   10

185. What is the name of the machine used to resurface the ice between periods?

(A)   Calzone

(B)   Giabrone

(C)   Zimbabwe

(D)   Zamboni

186. What was the significance of Manon Rheaume's appearance with the Tampa Bay Lightning in a 1992 preseason game against the St. Louis Blues in 1992?

(A)   Rheaume is a woman and that was the first appearance of a woman in a men's major professional sport league.

(B)   Rheaume is blind, but played goalie.

(C)   Rheaume has prosthetic legs, but played goalie.

(D)   Rheaume was still in high school.

187. What rival hockey league competed against the NHL from 1972 to 1979?

(A) NHA

(B) WHA

(C) AHA

(D) WHL

188. For which team did the "Broad Street Bullies" play in the 1970s?

(A) Chicago Blackhawks

(B) Detroit Red Wings

(C) Philadelphia Flyers

(D) New York Rangers

189. Who replaced Sid Abel on the famous "Production Line"?

(A) Phil Esposito

(B) Alex Delvecchio

(C) Bobby Orr

(D) Tim Horton

190. Which of the following was *not* a goalie?

(A) Doug Harvey

(B) Terry Sawchuk

(C) Jacques Plante

(D) Glenn Hall

191. Hobey Baker is the model for the literary character Allenby in *This Side of Paradise*, a novel written by which of the following authors?

(A) William Faulkner

(B) John Steinbeck

(C) F. Scott Fitzgerald

(D) John Grisham

192. Who was nicknamed "the Pocket Rocket"?

   (A) Maurice Richard

   (B) Henri Richard

   (C) Chris Chelios

   (D) Teemu Selanne

193. What is unusual about the Stanley Cup?

   (A) After the winning team wins it, a new one is made for the next year.

   (B) The original was lost in 1969 and a replica has been used ever since.

   (C) Each member of the winning team gets to take it home for a day.

   (D) Lord Stanley's ashes are in the cup, which is actually an urn.

194. What Tampa Bay Lightning player scored the Stanley Cup-winning goal in 2004?

   (A) Martin St. Louis

   (B) Cory Stillman

   (C) Ruslan Fedotenko

   (D) Andre Roy

195. Vladimir Krutov, Igor Larianov, and Sergei Makarov formed a line called which of the following?

   (A) "The Russian Line"

   (B) "The Soviet Line"

   (C) "The KGB Line"

   (D) "The KLM Line"

196. Which family had the most players in the NHL?

   (A) Sutter

   (B) Orr

   (C) Hull

   (D) Richard

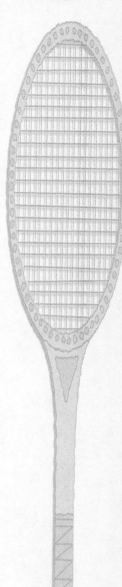

197. The youngest player in NHL history, Armand Guidolin, was how old when he started playing for the Boston Bruins in 1942?

(A) 12

(B) 14

(C) 16

(D) 18

198. The longest game in the NHL history lasted how long into overtime?

(A) 87 minutes and 30 seconds

(B) 97 minutes and 30 seconds

(C) 104 minutes and 30 seconds

(D) 116 minutes and 30 seconds

199. A famous playoff game between the Boston Bruins and the New Jersey Devils officiated by replacement officials in 1988 was known as which of the following?

(A) "Scrub a Dub Dub"

(B) "Yellow Sunday"

(C) "Scab Day"

(D) "The Joke"

200. How many NHL records does Wayne Gretzky hold or share?

(A) 45

(B) 50

(C) 55

(D) 61

201. Which of the following is a record that Wayne Gretzky does *not* hold?

(A) Most career goals

(B) Most career assists

(C) Most points by a defenseman in a season

(D) Most seasons of 40 or more goals

202. Which award is given to the outstanding goaltender each year?

(A) The Hart Memorial Trophy

(B) The Vezina Trophy

(C) The King Clancy Trophy

(D) The Conn Smythe Trophy

203. Who holds the record for most years in the Stanley Cup playoffs?

(A) Larry Robinson

(B) Larry Murphy

(C) Ray Bourque

(D) Gordie Howe

204. Which goaltender has appeared in the most Stanley Cup playoff games?

(A) Patrick Roy

(B) Grant Fuhr

(C) Ed Belfour

(D) Mike Vernon

205. Who was the 2004 NHL Rookie of the Year?

(A) Andrew Raycroft

(B) Barrett Jackman

(C) Trent Hunter

(D) Alexander Orechkin

CHAPTER 4 ANSWERS

155. The correct answer is (D). When a player scores three goals in a game, it is called a hat trick; a *natural hat trick* is three consecutive goals.

156. The correct answer is (D). In keeping with a tradition that began in 1952, it is quite common for fans to toss an octopus onto the ice at Red Wings games. The first octopus was thrown onto the ice by two brothers, Pete and Jerry Cusimano (who owned a fish store). Each of the eight tentacles represented the amount of playoff wins it took in 1952 to win the Stanley Cup.

157. The correct answer is (A). When the Stanley Cup became the property of the NHL, these were the only six cities in the league.

158. The correct answer is (B). In February 1934, the NHL held its first All-Star Game as a benefit for injured star Ace Bailey. Toronto defeated a team of All-Stars from the leagues other seven teams, 7–3.

159. The correct answer is (B). The U.S. hockey team upset the heavily-favored Soviets to win the gold in Lake Placid in 1980.

160. The correct answer is (D). There are a total of nine face-off spots on the ice, and the one used for a face-off depends on what action led to the face-off.

161. The correct answer is (A). According to the NHL rule book, a goalie cannot be a team captain, nor can a playing coach or manager.

162. The correct answer is (D). The "rookie of the year" award, the Calder Memorial Trophy, is named after Frank Calder, the NHL's first president.

163. The correct answer is (D). Howe was 51 years old when he played in his final All-Star Game in 1980, which was his twenty-third All-Star Game.

164. The correct answer is (B). Maurice "Rocket" Richard scored 50 goals in the 1944–45 season at a time when no one else had ever scored more than 45 goals.

165. **The correct answer is (C).** A jersey is often referred to as a sweater because in the early days of organized hockey, players wore sweaters and not jerseys.

166. **The correct answer is (B).** Since the 1973–74 season, all goalies have worn masks.

167. **The correct answer is (D).** Paul Coffey, who won the Norris Trophy three times, is considered one of the greatest defensemen of all-time.

168. **The correct answer is (D).** Mike Bossy, one of the most prolific goal scorers of all-time, was often called "The Boss" and "The Goal Machine."

169. **The correct answer is (B).** Hobey Baker, the namesake of the award, was a standout in both football and hockey in college at Princeton.

170. **The correct answer is (C).** The "Production Line" was a feature of many Red Wings teams in the late 1940s and beyond.

171. **The correct answer is (D).** Johnny Bucyk scored 50 goals at the age of 35, making him the oldest player to do so.

172. **The correct answer is (A).** Maurice Richard broke Abel's nose so badly that Abel became known as "Old Bootnose" after the fight.

173. **The correct answer is (D).** The Buffalo Sabres, led by the "French Connection" line, went to the Stanley Cup Finals in 1975 only a few years after coming into the league.

174. **The correct answer is (B).** Borje Salming was a defenseman from Sweden who played for 16 seasons with the Maple Leafs and one season with the Red Wings.

175. **The correct answer is (B).** Except for 1988, Wayne Gretzky won all the Hart Trophies of the 1980s.

176. **The correct answer is (C).** Teemu Selanne scored 76 goals as a rookie, 23 more than Bossy had scored as a rookie.

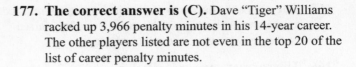

177. The correct answer is (C). Dave "Tiger" Williams racked up 3,966 penalty minutes in his 14-year career. The other players listed are not even in the top 20 of the list of career penalty minutes.

178. The correct answer is (D). Geoffrion is credited with the invention and use of the slap shot, now a common shot in hockey.

179. The correct answer is (C). The Montreal Canadiens have made 32 finals appearances, the most of any NHL team.

180. The correct answer is (A). The "pipe" is the goalpost. Therefore, if a player scores a goal, he has hit the puck "between the pipes."

181. The correct answer is (D). Craig MacTavish played without a helmet until he retired after the 1996–97 season.

182. The correct answer is (D). In thirty seasons as coach, Scotty Bowman notched 1244 wins—300 more wins than the next coach on the list has.

183. The correct answer is (B). The Hockey Hall of Fame and Museum is located in Toronto, Canada.

184. The correct answer is (C). Joe Malone scored seven goals in a game in 1920. Four times a player has dished out seven assists, and three of these times the assists were by Wayne Gretzky.

185. The correct answer is (D). The Zamboni, named for its creator, scrapes the ice and sprays a new layer of water on the surface of the ice making it smoother.

186. The correct answer is (A). Manon Rheaume was the first woman to appear in a men's major professional sport league.

187. The correct answer is (B). The WHA, or World Hockey Association, eventually folded and four teams merged with the NHL.

188. **The correct answer is (C).** Players like Dave "The Hammer" Schultz and Bobby Clarke, members of the "Broad Street Bullies," played for the rough-and-tumble Philadelphia Flyers.

189. **The correct answer is (B).** Alex Delvecchio replaced Sid Abel in the "Production Line" in 1952.

190. **The correct answer is (A).** Doug Harvey was a standout defenseman for the Montreal Canadiens.

191. **The correct answer is (C).** F. Scott Fitzgerald was so fascinated by Baker that he based one of his characters on him.

192. **The correct answer is (B).** Henri Richard, little brother of Maurice "the Rocket" Richard, was fittingly nicknamed "the Pocket Rocket."

193. **The correct answer is (C).** Each member of the winning team and the winning team's management get to take the trophy home for a day to share with family and friends.

194. **The correct answer is (C).** Ruslan Fedotenko, in game 7, scored both goals for the Tampa Bay Lightning in a 2–1 victory over the Calgary Flames that delivered the franchise its first Stanley Cup.

195. **The correct answer is (D).** The three Soviet players made up the "KLM Line" and were all eventually drafted by NHL teams.

196. **The correct answer is (A).** Six Sutter brothers all played in the NHL: Ron, Rich, Duane, Darryl, Brian, and Brent.

197. **The correct answer is (C).** Guidolin was 16 when he started playing, and he played for eleven years.

198. **The correct answer is (D).** The Detroit Red Wings defeated the Montreal Maroons 1–0 in the 117th minute of overtime in 1936.

199. The correct answer is (B). "Yellow Sunday" was called such because the replacement officials wore yellow practice jerseys instead of regular officials' shirts.

200. The correct answer is (D). The Great One holds or shares an unbelievable 61 NHL records.

201. The correct answer is (C). Gretzky was a center, so he was not a defenseman.

202. The correct answer is (B). The Vezina Trophy, named after a former Canadien goaltender, is given each year to the league's outstanding goaltender.

203. The correct answer is (C). Ray Borque has appeared in the Stanley Cup playoffs twenty-one times with Boston and Colorado.

204. The correct answer is (A). Patrick Roy has appeared in well over 200 playoff games, more than 80 more playoff games than the next goaltender on the list.

205. The correct answer is (A). The 2004 NHL Rookie of the Year was Boston Bruins goaltender Andrew Raycroft. He had a 2.05 goals-against average and a .926 save percentage in 57 games.

CHAPTER 5

Running on Full Throttle:
Auto Racing

206. Who is known as the "Patron Saint of NASCAR"?

   (A)   William "Bill" France

   (B)   Bill Elliott

   (C)   Jeff Gordon

   (D)   Rusty Wallace

207. Who qualified for the Indy 500 an amazing 35 consecutive times between 1958 and 1992?

   (A)   Mario Andretti

   (B)   Aldo Andretti

   (C)   A. J. Foyt

   (D)   Al Unser

> You've got to have a lead dog. You've got to have somebody out there for everyone to shoot at.
> —RICHARD PETTY

208. Who was the youngest driver to win the Daytona 500 twice?

   (A)   Mark Martin

   (B)   Kyle Petty

   (C)   Bill Elliott

   (D)   Jeff Gordon

209. Who is simply known as "the King"?

   (A)   Mario Andretti

   (B)   Al Unser

   (C)   Richard Petty

   (D)   Darrell Waltrip

210. Which of the following is true of the Indianapolis Motor Speedway?

   (A)   There are no public bathrooms at the facility.

   (B)   There is seating for nearly 100,000 fans.

   (C)   There is seating for about 300,000 fans.

   (D)   Horse-drawn carriages once raced on the track.

211. Shirley Muldowney made racing history in which type of auto racing?

   (A)   Indy Cars

   (B)   NASCAR

   (C)   Drag Racing

   (D)   None of the above

212. Who was the first NHRA driver to surpass 300 miles per hour in the quarter mile?

   (A)   Kenny Bernstein

   (B)   Shirley Muldowney

   (C)   Don Garlits

   (D)   John Force

213. Which of the following drivers raced the final race of his life at the Daytona 500 in 2001?

(A) Al Unser

(B) Dale Earnhardt Sr.

(C) Richard Petty

(D) None of the above

214. Who besides Richard Petty has won the Daytona 500 two years in a row?

(A) Jeff Gordon

(B) Kyle Petty

(C) David Pearson

(D) Cale Yarborough

215. What do A. J. Foyt, Al Unser, and Rick Mears share as a career accomplishment?

(A) Four Coca-Cola 600 victories each

(B) Four Indy 500 victories each

(C) A NASCAR championship and an NHRA championship each

(D) Breaking the 350 mile per hour barrier in the quarter mile

216. Which of the following drivers once competed in the Indy 500 and in a Winston Cup race on the same day?

(A) Mario Andretti

(B) Aldo Andretti

(C) John Andretti

(D) Richard Petty

217. What race venue is also known as "the Brickyard"?

(A) Daytona

(B) Talladega

(C) Rockingham

(D) Indianapolis Motor Speedway

218. Which of the following is the name of Al Unser's brother, a successful driver at Indianapolis Motor Speedway?

(A) Mel

(B) Joe

(C) Bobby

(D) Billy

219. In what year did a driver wear the first protective helmet at the Indy 500?

(A) 1929

(B) 1939

(C) 1949

(D) 1959

220. Which driver has earned the nickname "King of the Ovals" (not to be confused with "the King")?

(A) Mario Andretti

(B) Rick Mears

(C) Bobby Johns

(D) Cale Yarborough

221. Which country is the homeland of driver Jackie Stewart?

(A) England

(B) Ireland

(C) Scotland

(D) Australia

222. Who was the first woman to qualify for the Indy 500?

(A) Lyn St. James

(B) Shirley Muldowney

(C) Janet Guthrie

(D) Stella Lombardi

223. A rookie driver can be spotted at Indianapolis because of which of the following distinguishing marks on his car?

   (A) The word "rookie" on the tail of the car

   (B) The word "rookie" on the hood of the car

   (C) The driver wears a yellow and orange helmet

   (D) Three stripes on either side of the tail of the car

224. Which of the following, one of America's best known Formula One drivers, has a father who was an opera star?

   (A) Dan Gurney

   (B) Emerson Fittipaldi

   (C) A. J. Foyt

   (D) Jim Clark

225. Who was the oldest person to ever win the Daytona 500?

   (A) Al Unser

   (B) Cale Yarborough

   (C) Bobby Allison

   (D) Richard Petty

226. What racer goes by the nickname of "Big Daddy"?

   (A) Dan Gurney

   (B) Don Garlits

   (C) Ricky Rudd

   (D) Dale Earnhardt, Sr.

227. Which of the following safety accessories was reportedly first used at Indianapolis Motor Speedway?

   (A) Seat belts

   (B) Turn signals

   (C) Safety goggles

   (D) Rearview mirrors

228. Robert "Junior" Johnson spent eleven months in federal prison because of a conviction for which of the following?

(A) Bank robbery

(B) Stealing a car

(C) Drag racing

(D) Running moonshine

229. Who unsuccessfully ran for the position of North Carolina's Secretary of State in 1996?

(A) Richard Petty

(B) Kyle Petty

(C) Roger Penske

(D) Lyn St. James

230. Who is the only driver to be World Champion, winner of the 24 Hour Le Mans, and winner of the Indy 500?

(A) Graham Hill

(B) A. J. Foyt

(C) Emerson Fittipaldi

(D) Jackie Stewart

231. Who is the only driver in history to win the 24 Hour Le Mans, the Indy 500, and the Daytona 500?

(A) Graham Hill

(B) A. J. Foyt

(C) Emerson Fittipaldi

(D) Jackie Stewart

232. Driver Emerson Fittipaldi was born in which of the following countries?

(A) England

(B) Scotland

(C) Brazil

(D) Argentina

233. Which race traditionally begins with "Gentlemen, start your engines"?

   (A)   Indianapolis 500

   (B)   Brickyard 400

   (C)   Daytona 500

   (D)   Australian Grand Prix

234. Which father/son duo was the first to win the NASCAR championship?

   (A)   Buck and Buddy Baker

   (B)   Ralph and Dale Earnhardt

   (C)   Ned and Dale Jarrett

   (D)   Richard and Lee Petty

235. Who was the Formula One champion for 2003 and 2004?

   (A)   Alain Prost

   (B)   Aldo Andretti

   (C)   Michael Schumacher

   (D)   Juan Pablo Montoya

236. What NASCAR driver was dubbed "Boy Wonder" and "Rainbow Warrior"?

   (A)   Tony Stewart

   (B)   Mark Martin

   (C)   Rusty Wallace

   (D)   Jeff Gordon

237. What is the average time of a NASCAR pitstop?

   (A)   Less than 20 seconds

   (B)   30 seconds

   (C)   40 seconds

   (D)   1 minute

238. When did the NASCAR Craftsman Truck Series begin?

  (A) 1965

  (B) 1975

  (C) 1985

  (D) 1995

239. Who is the oldest driver to win the Winston Cup Rookie of the Year award?

  (A) Bobby Allison

  (B) Cale Yarborough

  (C) Dick Trickle

  (D) Lake Speed

240. Which racing family makes up the "Alabama Gang"?

  (A) The Pettys

  (B) The Allisons

  (C) The Yarboroughs

  (D) The Andrettis

241. Which of the following was the first person to drive at a speed of a mile a minute?

  (A) Barney Oldfield

  (B) Bill France

  (C) Dan Gurney

  (D) Alain Prost

242. Who was the first stock car driver to reach the $1,000,000 earnings mark in his career?

  (A) Lee Roy Yarborough

  (B) Ned Jarrett

  (C) Buck Baker

  (D) Richard Petty

243. Who was the subject of a biographical movie in 1983 called "Heart Like a Wheel"?

    (A) Richard Petty

    (B) Bill France

    (C) Shirley Muldowney

    (D) Roger Penske

244. A "funny car" would most likely be found at which of the following races?

    (A) A Formula One race

    (B) A drag race

    (C) A NASCAR race

    (D) An Indy race

245. Who was the NASCAR Winston Cup champion for 2003?

    (A) Tony Stewart

    (B) Dale Earnhardt Jr.

    (C) Matt Kenseth

    (D) Jeff Gordon

246. Top fuel dragsters usually run the quarter mile in approximately how many seconds?

    (A) 7–8

    (B) 6–7

    (C) 5–6

    (D) 4–5

247. What driver won the Winston Cup championship seven times, but in his first 19 tries at Daytona never finished better than second?

    (A) Dale Jarrett

    (B) Dale Earnhardt

    (C) Rusty Wallace

    (D) Ernie Ervan

248. What happened at the end of the 1979 Daytona 500 that was televised in its entirety on national TV?

(A) A crash prevented the officials from declaring a winner.

(B) Richard Petty crashed and spun around as he crossed the finish line.

(C) The power went out at the TV station and the nation missed the end of the race.

(D) Donnie Allison and Cale Yarborough got into a fight after their crash, which allowed Richard Petty to steal the race.

249. What is the relatively new racing league that competes with CART/Indy Car?

(A) NASCAR

(B) IROC

(C) IRL

(D) NHRA

250. What problem did Jackie Stewart have to overcome in order to be a successful race car driver?

(A) Nearsightedness

(B) Farsightedness

(C) ADD

(D) Dyslexia

251. Ray Harround won the very first Indy 500 in 1911 with what time?

(A) 3 hours and 42 minutes

(B) 4 hours and 42 minutes

(C) 5 hours and 42 minutes

(D) 6 hours and 42 minutes

252. Traditionally, the winner of the Indy 500 drinks what beverage in Victory Lane?

(A) Beer

(B) Champagne

(C) Milk

(D) Gatorade

253. What is the closest Winston Cup finish in history?

(A) 6 seconds

(B) .6 seconds

(C) .06 seconds

(D) .006 seconds

254. Who held the record for most consecutive NASCAR races started until 2000?

(A) Richard Petty

(B) Terry Labonte

(C) Ricky Rudd

(D) Dale Earnhardt

255. How many cars are allowed to participate in the Indianapolis 500?

(A) 15

(B) 24

(C) 33

(D) 42

256. Who was the first driver to win the Daytona 500, the Indy 500, and win the Formula One championship?

(A) Mario Andretti

(B) Dan Gurney

(C) Jackie Stewart

(D) Richard Petty

CHAPTER 5 ANSWERS

206. **The correct answer is (A).** William France founded the National Association of Stock Car Auto Racing in 1947. When someone is called the "patron saint" of something, it usually implies that one is a founder. Choices (B), (C), and (D) raced in the 2002 season, so you could guess that they are probably not founders.

207. **The correct answer is (C).** Foyt, one of the greatest Indy drivers of all time, qualified for 35 consecutive Indianapolis 500 races.

208. **The correct answer is (D).** Jeff Gordon was not only the youngest driver to win the Daytona 500 twice, but he was also the youngest driver to earn 50 wins.

209. **The correct answer is (C).** The great Richard Petty is known simply as "the King." He has 200 NASCAR wins to his name, more than 700 top 10 finishes, and has won 7 Winston Cup championships.

210. **The correct answer is (C).** The Indianapolis Motor Speedway, the largest sporting venue in the U.S., can hold more than 300,000 fans.

211. **The correct answer is (C).** Muldowney began drag racing in 1965 and has won numerous titles and championships, despite being far outnumbered by her male competitors. She won the National Hot Rod Association World Championships in 1977, 1980, and 1982.

212. **The correct answer is (A).** Kenny Bernstein, one of the NHRA's top drivers, was the first to reach the 300 miles per hour plateau in the quarter mile.

213. **The correct answer is (B).** Dale Earnhardt Sr. was tragically killed while racing in the 2001 Daytona 500. He raced on the NASCAR circuit for 22 years, had 76 career wins, 7 Winston Cup championships, and made more money racing than any other NASCAR driver.

214. **The correct answer is (D).** Cale Yarborough won the Daytona 500 in 1983 and 1984.

215. The correct answer is (B). Foyt, Unser, and Mears are the only drivers with four Indy 500 victories each.

216. The correct answer is (C). John Andretti competed in the Indy 500 in May 1994, and he then flew to North Carolina where he competed in the Coca-Cola 600 later that same day.

217. The correct answer is (D). The original track, which opened in 1909, was laid with more than 3,000,000 bricks.

218. The correct answer is (C). Al Unser's successful racing brother is named Bobby. Bobby Unser won numerous awards, including Indy 500 wins in 1968 and 1975, and has 12 wins at the Pikes Peak Hill Climb, among other career wins.

219. The correct answer is (A). According to records, Louis Chiron wore the first crash helmet in 1929.

220. The correct answer is (B). Because of his many successes on the track, Rick Mears is often referred to as the "King of the Ovals."

221. The correct answer is (C). Jackie Stewart was born in Scotland.

222. The correct answer is (C). Janet Guthrie was the first woman to qualify for the Indy 500, and she first raced there in 1977. She finished in ninth place the next year at Indy, which is the highest finish by a woman driver ever recorded.

223. The correct answer is (D). At Indianapolis, rookie drivers are marked with three stripes on either side of the tail of their cars.

224. The correct answer is (A). Daniel "Dan" Gurney's father was a famous Metropolitan Opera star.

225. The correct answer is (C). In 1988, Bobby Allison won the Daytona 500 at the age of 50.

226. The correct answer is (B). NHRA racer Don Garlits often goes by "Big Daddy."

227. The correct answer is (D). Rearview mirrors were first used at the Indianapolis Motor Speedway.

228. The correct answer is (D). Junior Johnson spent eleven months in federal prison in 1956 for running moonshine. He retired at the age of 34 from NASCAR with more than fifty victories and went on to become a successful car owner.

229. The correct answer is (A). Richard Petty ran for, but was not elected to, the office of Secretary of State in North Carolina.

230. The correct answer is (A). Graham Hill is the only driver to be World Champion, winner of the Indy 500, and the 24 Hour Le Mans.

231. The correct answer is (B). A. J. Foyt is the only driver to win the Indy 500, the Daytona 500, and the 24 Hour Le Mans.

232. The correct answer is (C). Emerson "Emo" Fittipaldi is Brazilian.

233. The correct answer is (A). For years, the Indy 500 has begun with the phrase, "Gentlemen, start your engines," which is one of the most familiar phrases in all of sports.

234. The correct answer is (D). The Pettys were the first father and son duo to win the NASCAR championship.

235. The correct answer is (C). Michael Schumacher, from Germany, won his sixth world championship in 2003. This broke the tie with Juan Manuel Fangio for the most Formula One titles. Schumacher won his seventh world championship in 2004.

236. The correct answer is (D). Jeff Gordon earned the nickname "Boy Wonder" after his successful rookie season and the nickname "Rainbow Warrior" because of his brightly painted car.

237. The correct answer is (A). The average NASCAR pitstop takes less than 20 seconds and includes a fill-up and four new tires.

238. **The correct answer is (D).** Mike Skinner beat out Terry Labonte to win the first race in 1995.

239. **The correct answer is (C).** In 1989, Dick Trickle won the award at the age of 48.

240. **The correct answer is (B).** The notorious "Alabama Gang" is composed of the Allison family racers.

241. **The correct answer is (A).** Barney Oldfield was the first to drive 60 miles per hour on June 15, 1903 at Indianapolis; he was also suspended for life from the American Automobile Association (AAA) for his outlaw racing (racing not sanctioned by the AAA) in 1910 only to be reinstated in 1912.

242. **The correct answer is (D).** Richard Petty reached the million dollar plateau long before any other stock car driver.

243. **The correct answer is (C).** "Heart Like a Wheel" was about 3-time NHRA champion Shirley Muldowney.

244. **The correct answer is (B).** A funny car is a type of car used in drag racing.

245. **The correct answer is (C).** Matt Kenseth won his first Cup championship in 2003. It was the first ever championship for the team owner.

246. **The correct answer is (C).** Top Fuel dragsters typically run the quarter mile in 5–6 seconds; the record for the quarter mile is under 5 seconds.

247. **The correct answer is (B).** Dale Earnhardt finished second at Daytona four times, in the top 10 five times, and then finally won Daytona in 1998.

248. **The correct answer is (D).** Donnie Allison and Cale Yarborough crashed into each other in the last lap and they fell out of contention. Richard Petty won the race. After the race, Yarborough and Allison got in a fight with the entire nation watching.

249. **The correct answer is (C).** In 1996, the Indy Racing League (IRL) was formed. Most big name drivers race in CART/Indy Car and not in the IRL.

250. The correct answer is (D). Jackie Stewart had to learn how to cope with his dyslexia in order to get through school and ultimately become one of racing's greatest stars.

251. The correct answer is (D). Compared to today's races, Ray Harround's 6 hours and 42 minutes seems like a snail's pace.

252. The correct answer is (C). The winner usually drinks milk because, in 1936, Louis Meyer won the Indy 500 and he was photographed gulping down buttermilk after the race, at the suggestion of his mother. The Milk Foundation then began using that as a forum for promoting milk, and from then on ensured that the winners of the Indy 500 always drank milk after the race.

253. The correct answer is (D). In 2001, Kevin Harvick *narrowly* beat Jeff Gordon in Atlanta by .006 seconds.

254. The correct answer is (B). At last count, Terry Labonte had 655 consecutive starts.

255. The correct answer is (C). Only 33 cars are allowed on the Indy track because each car is given 400 feet of track and there is 13,200 feet of track at Indy.

256. The correct answer is (A). Mario Andretti was already a Daytona 500 winner, Sebring winner, two-time USAC champion, and a four-time Indianapolis 500 competitor when he entered his first Formula One race in 1968. His first win on the Formula One circuit came in 1971 in South Africa.

CHAPTER 6

The Galloping Ghost and Chocolate Thunder:
Nicknames

257. What basketball player was known as "Air"?

(A) Larry Bird

(B) Oscar Robertson

(C) Michael Jordan

(D) Scottie Pippen

258. What two baseball players were known as the "Bash Brothers"?

A) Mickey Mantle and Roger Maris

(B) Hank Aaron and Eddie Matthews

(C) Hank Aaron and Tommie Aaron

(D) Jose Canseco and Mark McGwire

> Do we define our nicknames, or are we defined by our nicknames?
> —ANONYMOUS

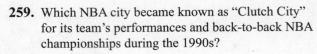
259. Which NBA city became known as "Clutch City" for its team's performances and back-to-back NBA championships during the 1990s?

(A) Chicago

(B) Los Angeles

(C) Boston

(D) Houston

260. "Mr. October" is the nickname once given to whom?

(A) Babe Ruth

(B) Mike Schmidt

(C) Dale Murphy

(D) Reggie Jackson

261. What baseball player was known as "Charlie Hustle"?

(A) Pete Rose

(B) Charlie Hough

(C) Charlie Hayes

(D) Len Dykstra

262. Which basketball player entered the NBA with the nickname "Penny"?

(A) Anfernee Hardaway

(B) Tim Hardaway

(C) Kenny Smith

(D) Scottie Pippen

263. In the *Rocky* movie series, Rocky Balboa was known as what?

(A) "Balboa the Boa"

(B) "Cocky Rocky"

(C) "The Thrilla from Manilla"

(D) "The Italian Stallion"

264. Which 1970s NFL franchise had a group of players known as the "Purple People Eaters"?

(A) New York Giants

(B) Minnesota Vikings

(C) San Diego Chargers

(D) Chicago Bears

265. NHL great Wayne Gretzky is often referred to as which of the following?

(A) "Insane Wayne"

(B) "Gretzky the Great"

(C) "The Great Gretzky"

(D) "The Great One"

266. The Australian golfer Greg Norman has earned which nickname?

(A) "The Putter from Down Under"

(B) "The Koala"

(C) "Stormin' Norman"

(D) "The Shark"

267. Who was "The Great Bambino"?

(A) George Foreman

(B) Mickey Mantle

(C) Charles Barkley

(D) Babe Ruth

268. "Broadway" was often added to the beginning of whose name during his NFL career?

(A) Joe Montana

(B) Joe Namath

(C) Jim Brown

(D) Barry Sanders

269. Which NFL stadium boasts the "Frozen Tundra"?

(A) Chicago's Soldier Field

(B) Kansas City's Arrowhead Stadium

(C) Green Bay's Lambeau Field

(D) Dallas's Texas Stadium

270. "The Round Mound of Rebound" is a term of endearment for which NBA player?

(A) Charles Barkley

(B) Shaquille O'Neal

(C) Antoine Carr

(D) Bill Russell

271. Roger Clemens is often referred to as which of the following powerful nicknames?

(A) "The Cannon"

(B) "The Ripper"

(C) "The Rocket"

(D) "The Catapult"

272. A Green Bay Packers fan can be called a "Packer Backer" or what other nickname?

(A) "Green Bay Groupie"

(B) "A member of the Pack pack"

(C) "Lambeau Loyalist"

(D) "Cheesehead"

273. Which NCAA school has "Cameron Crazies" that attend its basketball games and make lots of noise to distract visiting teams?

(A) Duke

(B) North Carolina

(C) Michigan State

(D) UCLA

274. Hank Aaron often had which of the following prefixes added to his name?

(A) "Homer"

(B) "Homer Hitter"

(C) "Homerun"

(D) "Hammerin"

275. Which of the following nicknames was given to Julius Erving during his professional basketball career?

(A) "Magic"

(B) "Dr. J"

(C) "Dr. Dunk"

(D) "Sterling"

276. "The Tribe" is a nickname given to which of the following pro teams?

(A) Washington Redskins

(B) Cleveland Indians

(C) Chicago Blackhawks

(D) Atlanta Braves

277. "Sweetness" was the nickname of which great running back?

(A) Walter Payton

(B) Barry Sanders

(C) Earl Campbell

(D) John Riggins

278. "Chocolate Thunder" was the nickname of which high-flying slam-dunker?

(A) Dominique Wilkins

(B) Dee Brown

(C) Julius Erving

(D) Darryl Dawkins

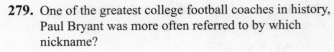

279. One of the greatest college football coaches in history, Paul Bryant was more often referred to by which nickname?

(A) "Butch"

(B) "Bo"

(C) "Bear"

(D) "Boomer"

280. The "Dome Patrol" was the linebacking corps of which professional football team in the 1990s?

(A) Minnesota Vikings

(B) Houston Oilers

(C) Atlanta Falcons

(D) New Orleans Saints

281. Joe Jackson, probably one of the only innocent members of the 1919 Chicago White Sox, is famous for which of the following nicknames?

(A) "Jumpin' Joe Jackson"

(B) "Jolly Joe Jackson"

(C) "Speedy Joe Jackson"

(D) "Shoeless Joe Jackson"

282. Atlanta Braves star "Chipper" Jones' real first name is which of the following?

(A) Jason

(B) Jacques

(C) Andruw

(D) Larry

283. "The Golden Bear" is the nickname of which golf legend?

(A) Jack Nicklaus

(B) Tiger Woods

(C) Arnold Palmer

(D) Sam Snead

284. Boxing great Sonny Liston earned what fitting nickname?

(A) "The Drummer Boy"

(B) "Not-so-funny Sonny"

(C) "Liston the Piston"

(D) "Clubber Liston"

285. The first name of part-time philosopher Yogi Berra is actually which of the following?

(A) Yani

(B) Billy

(C) Lawrence

(D) B.B.

286. "The Golden Jet" was the nickname of which hockey great?

(A) Wayne Gretzky

(B) Bobby Hull

(C) Brett Hull

(D) Gordie Howe

287. "The Say Hey Kid" is the name of which Hall of Fame baseball player?

(A) Hank Aaron

(B) Jackie Robinson

(C) Brooks Robinson

(D) Willie Mays

288. Los Angeles Lakers icon Jerry West was given what unusual nickname?

(A) Scary Jerry

(B) The Compass

(C) Zeke from Cabin Creek

(D) The Wicked Witch of the West

289. "The Snake" was the nickname of which NFL quarterback?

(A) Ken Stabler

(B) Dan Pastorini

(C) Archie Manning

(D) Fran Tarkenton

290. Which Cub was known as "The Hawk"?

(A) Ernie Banks

(B) Ryne Sandberg

(C) Mark Grace

(D) Andre Dawson

291. Chuck Person earned which nickname for his shooting expertise in the NBA?

(A) "Deadeye"

(B) "Bullseye"

(C) "The Cannon"

(D) "The Rifleman"

292. Also referred to as "Jaws," Ron Jaworski garnered which other nickname during his NFL career?

(A) "The Polish Sausage"

(B) "The Polish Rifle"

(C) "The Polish Bomber"

(D) "The Polish Prowler"

293. Which pitcher, perhaps best known for his antics on the mound, was known as "The Bird"?

(A) Rich Gossage

(B) Ron Guidry

(C) Mark Fydrich

(D) Tom Seaver

294. NBA star Eric Floyd shared which nickname with one of the Seven Dwarves?

(A) "Grumpy"

(B) "Sleepy"

(C) "Doc"

(D) "Happy"

295. "The General" refers to which formidable coach?

(A) Paul Bryant

(B) Adolph Rupp

(C) Pat Summitt

(D) Bobby Knight

296. Which college football team's stadium is overlooked by a large mural nicknamed "Touchdown Jesus"?

(A) Notre Dame

(B) Boston College

(C) Stanford

(D) Baylor

297. Although "Butterbean" could refer to a wrestler, it usually refers to which famous basketball player?

(A) Bill Russell

(B) Bob Love

(C) Charles Barkley

(D) James Worthy

298. "The Galloping Ghost" is the nickname of which throwback football great?

(A) Larry Csonka

(B) Bronko Nagurski

(C) Knute Rockne

(D) Red Grange

299. Ty Cobb once went by which ironic nickname?

(A) "The Georgia Peach"

(B) "Sunshine"

(C) "Cy"

(D) "The Blob"

300. Which professional athlete has often been called "Super Mex"?

(A) Oscar de la Hoya

(B) Fernando Valenzuela

(C) Tony Gonzalez

(D) Lee Trevino

301. Which U.S. Supreme Court justice and former football star was known as "Whizzer"?

(A) Antonin Scalia

(B) Byron White

(C) Oliver Wendell Holmes

(D) Warren Berger

302. "The Old Perfessor's" real name is which of the following?

(A) Yogi Berra

(B) Joe McCarthy

(C) Charles "Casey" Stengel

(D) Joe Torre

303. Which of the following is NBA little-man "Muggsy" Bogues' real name?

(A) Bugsy

(B) Billy

(C) B.B.

(D) Tyrone

304. "The Egg Bowl" is the nickname for which of the following annual college football games?

(A) Ole Miss vs. Mississippi State

(B) Army vs. Navy

(C) Texas vs. Texas A&M

(D) Alabama vs. Auburn

305. What was hockey standout Derek Sanderson's nickname?

(A) "Turk"

(B) "The German"

(C) "The Russian"

(D) "The Canadian"

306. Track and Field great Paavo Nurmi is most famous as which of the following?

(A) "Bravo Paavo"

(B) "The Fastest Finn on Feet"

(C) "The Flying Finn"

(D) "The Rocket"

CHAPTER 6 ANSWERS

257. The correct answer is (C). Michael Jordan was dubbed "Air" Jordan during his days with the Chicago Bulls in the 1980s and 1990s.

258. The correct answer is (D). Jose Canseco and Mark McGwire reached celebrity status as the "Bash Brothers" during their time together with the Oakland A's because of all the home runs they hit.

259. The correct answer is (D). Houston became known as "Clutch City" because its Rockets came through in the clutch during two title runs in 1994 and 1995.

260. The correct answer is (D). Reggie Jackson was known as "Mr. October" for his incredible performances in the World Series including a three-homer game.

261. The correct answer is (A). Pete Rose's hustle, effort, and enthusiasm for the game of baseball earned him the nickname "Charlie Hustle."

262. The correct answer is (A). Anfernee Hardaway's grandmother called him "pretty," but it sounded like "penny," and that's what stuck with him.

263. The correct answer is (D). Rocky's nickname in the *Rocky* movies was "The Italian Stallion."

264. The correct answer is (B). During the 1970s, the Minnesota Vikings had a ferocious defense featuring Carl Eller, Gary Larsen, Alan Page, and Jim Marshall; they were known as the "Purple People Eaters"—the Vikings colors are purple and yellow.

265. The correct answer is (D). Often regarded as the greatest NHL player of all time, Wayne Gretzky is simply known as "The Great One."

266. The correct answer is (D). Greg Norman attributes his nickname, "The Shark," to a newspaper article written about him during the 1980s. A shark is the logo for Greg Norman apparrel.

267. The correct answer is (D). "The Great Bambino" is a nickname fitting only of a superstar like George Herman "Babe" Ruth.

268. **The correct answer is (B).** "Broadway" Joe Namath earned his nickname for his flamboyant, eccentric behavior during his days as a young quarterback for the New York Jets, including wearing a full-length fur coat on the sidelines.

269. **The correct answer is (C).** Because of its bitterly cold winters, Green Bay's Lambeau Field is affectionately referred to as the "Frozen Tundra."

270. **The correct answer is (A).** "Sir" Charles Barkley earned a new title, "The Round Mound of Rebound," for his great rebounding abilities despite his relatively short height for a great rebounder (6'4"–6'6" depending on who you believe!).

271. **The correct answer is (C).** Because of his overpowering fastball, Roger Clemens has been called "The Rocket" since his early days in Boston.

272. **The correct answer is (D).** Because of the huge dairy industry in Wisconsin, Green Bay (Wisconsin) Packers fans are known as "Cheeseheads"; they often wear large foam cheese wedges on their heads.

273. **The correct answer is (A).** Cameron Indoor Arena, home of Duke University's basketball teams, boasts some of the NCAA's best fans, the "Cameron Crazies."

274. **The correct answer is (D).** Because of the frequency and power with which he hit home runs, it was only fitting that Henry Aaron be known as "Hammerin' Hank Aaron."

275. **The correct answer is (B).** One of the greatest players and dunkers in basketball history, Julius Erving, was and is known simply as "Dr. J."

276. **The correct answer is (B).** Cleveland Indian fans often refer to their team as "The Tribe."

277. **The correct answer is (A).** For his grace both on and off the gridiron, "Sweetness" is the only nickname fitting for the legendary Walter Payton.

278. **The correct answer is (D).** Known for his monstrous, thunderous dunks, 14-year NBA veteran Darryl Dawkins earned the nickname "Chocolate Thunder."

279. The correct answer is (C). Legendary coach Paul Bryant, who coached football at Maryland, Kentucky, Texas A&M, and Alabama earned the nickname "Bear" by wrestling a bear at age fourteen in a local theatre for one dollar a minute.

280. The correct answer is (D). Vaughan Johnson, Pat Swilling, Sam Mills, and Rickey Jackson made up the New Orleans Saints linebacking corps known as the "Dome Patrol," because they played in the Superdome.

281. The correct answer is (D). "Shoeless" Joe Jackson was one of the members of the infamous Chicago Black Sox, and possibly the only member who didn't throw the World Series. He earned the nickname as a teenager playing for a local mill team—his feet were blistered from new shoes, and he couldn't wear his old shoes due to the pain, so he played in socks!

282. The correct answer is (D). "Chipper" Jones was actually born Larry Wayne Jones Jr.

283. The correct answer is (A). "The Golden Bear" is a nickname belonging to golfing legend Jack Nicklaus, because he was once described as "large, strong, blond, and growly."

284. The correct answer is (A). Boxer Sonny Liston earned the nickname "The Drummer Boy" because he reportedly beat his opponents the same way one would beat a drum.

285. The correct answer is (C). Baseball legend "Yogi" Berra, known for his profound statements, such as "it ain't over 'till it's over," was born as Lawrence Berra.

286. The correct answer is (B). Bobby Hull's blond hair and rugged good looks, combined, of course, with a devastating shot, earned him the nickname "The Golden Jet."

287. The correct answer is (D). Often considered one of baseball's all-time greatest players, Willie Mays is also known as "The Say Hey Kid," because of his enthusiasm for baseball.

288. The correct answer is (C). Jerry West always hated the nickname "Zeke from Cabin Creek." A reporter gave him that nickname because West was from Cabin Creek and Zeke was the only name the reporter could think of to rhyme with creek.

289. The correct answer is (A). Although Ken Stabler also played with the Oilers and the Saints, the nickname "Snake" best suited Stabler when he played with the Raiders. He earned the nickname in high school after a tremendous run; his coach said he ran "like a snake."

290. The correct answer is (D). Although he played with the Expos, Red Sox, and Marlins, Andre "The Hawk" Dawson is probably best remembered as a member of the Chicago Cubs.

291. The correct answer is (D). During his NBA days as a 3-point expert, Chuck Person was referred to simply as "The Rifleman." He got this nickname because his mother liked "The Rifleman," a western on TV that starred a former Celtics player.

292. The correct answer is (B). Ron Jaworski was dubbed "The Polish Rifle" by a newspaper because of his powerful throwing arm.

293. The correct answer is (C). Mark "The Bird" Fydrich first won fame with Rookie of the Year honors in 1976, and then became famous for his antics on the mound during the rest of his average career.

294. The correct answer is (B). Eric "Sleepy" Floyd certainly did not receive his nickname for his play on the court since he was one of the Houston Rockets' all-time great players.

295. The correct answer is (D). Known as "The General" as much for his leadership ability as for his strict command of his teams, Bobby Knight became a coaching legend at Indiana before moving on to Texas Tech.

296. The correct answer is (A). Notre Dame's football stadium has a clear view of a library building on campus that is decorated with a large mural known as "Touchdown Jesus."

297. The correct answer is (B). Louisiana native Bob Love was nicknamed "Butterbean" after his favorite food.

298. **The correct answer is (D).** Football legend Red Grange was called "The Galloping Ghost" because he was easily the best runner of his era.

299. **The correct answer is (A).** Ty Cobb, born in Northern Georgia, was given the nickname "The Georgia Peach," not because of his personality, but because of his birthplace.

300. **The correct answer is (D).** Lee Trevino often goes by his nickname "Super Mex" although he is actually from Texas and not from Mexico.

301. **The correct answer is (B).** Byron "Whizzer" White was a great football player at the University of Colorado and then went on to sign with Pittsburgh in 1938 for the largest player contract of his time, $15,800.

302. **The correct answer is (C).** Arguably the greatest manager of all time, "The Old Perfessor" Casey Stengel was known for great quotes and sayings.

303. **The correct answer is (D).** Long-time NBA star "Muggsy" Bogues was born Tyrone Bogues, and at 5'3" in height, Bogues is the shortest player to ever play in the NBA.

304. **The correct answer is (A).** The annual game between SEC rivals Mississippi State and Ole Miss is called "The Egg Bowl" because of the bitter rivalry between the two schools.

305. **The correct answer is (A).** Derek Sanderson, also known as "Turk," was one of the great players in Boston Bruins history.

306. **The correct answer is (C).** Paavo Nurmi won nine gold medals and three silver medals in the Olympics between 1920 and 1928 and was considered the greatest runner of his time. "The Flying Finn" was once banned from the Olympics by Finland to allow other Finnish runners a chance to win.

CHAPTER 7

Hear Me Roar:
Women in Sports

307. What dynamic gymnast became the first American woman to win the gold medal in the All-Around in women's Olympic gymnastics in 1984?

(A) Kerri Strug

(B) Mary Lou Retton

(C) Dominique Moceanu

(D) Shannon Miller

308. Which of the following women won 20 Wimbledon titles, 13 U.S. Open titles, the French Open, and the Australian Open in the 1960s, 1970s, and early 1980s, and helped organize the Virginia Slims women's tennis tour?

(A) Chris Evert

(B) Althea Gibson

(C) Billie Jean King

(D) Martina Navratilova

The formula for success is simple: practice and concentration, then more practice and more concentration.
—BABE DIDRIKSON ZAHARIAS

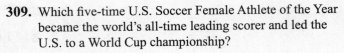

309. Which five-time U.S. Soccer Female Athlete of the Year became the world's all-time leading scorer and led the U.S. to a World Cup championship?

(A) Mia Hamm

(B) Brandi Chastain

(C) Michelle Akers

(D) Julie Foudy

310. What was the nickname of Mildred Didrikson Zaharias, a Texan who competed in professional golf, Olympic track and field, and even exhibition baseball and boxing?

(A) "Butch"

(B) "Barbie"

(C) "Barbells"

(D) "Babe"

311. Which gymnast, in the 1976 Summer Olympics, received the first-ever perfect 10?

(A) Cathy Rigby

(B) Olga Korbut

(C) Nadia Comaneci

(D) Mary Lou Retton

312. Which of the following women, by holding the record in the 100 meter dash and 200 meter dash, is considered the fastest woman in the world?

(A) Jackie Joyner-Kersee

(B) Wilma Rudolph

(C) Evelyn Ashford

(D) Florence Griffith-Joyner

313. Ashley Martin, the first woman to score in an NCAA Division I football game, did so in 2001 for which school?

(A) Florida State University

(B) University of North Carolina

(C) Baylor University

(D) Jacksonville State University

314. Dot Richardson became internationally known for leading her U.S. Olympic team to the gold medal in which of the following sports?

(A) Volleyball

(B) Softball

(C) Basketball

(D) Synchronized swimming

315. What legislation required collegiate athletic programs to offer financial aid and more athletic opportunities for women, thereby evening the playing field for female athletes in college?

(A) Proposition 48

(B) Public Law 94-142

(C) Title IX

(D) Chapter XIII

316. In order for a woman to be eligible for the LPGA Hall of Fame without having won any majors, she must have at least how many other tour wins?

(A) 25

(B) 30

(C) 35

(D) 40

317. In 1925, Gertrude Ederle became the first woman to do which of the following?

(A) Swim the English Channel

(B) Compete in a Boston Marathon

(C) Play in the major leagues

(D) Win a boxing title

318. Susan Butcher has won which of the following four times, more than any other male or female?

(A) Boston Marathon

(B) New York Marathon

(C) Iron Man Competition

(D) Iditarod

319. Who was the first female boxer to be televised on Pay-Per-View?

(A) Laila Ali

(B) Christy Martin

(C) Dianna Lewis

(D) Melinda Cooper

320. Which of the following tennis legends won 168 singles titles and 165 doubles titles in her career while being ranked #1 in the world for an amazing 223 weeks?

(A) Anna Kournikova

(B) Pam Shriver

(C) Martina Navratilova

(D) Tracy Austin

321. What was the first tournament Monica Seles won after returning to tennis from a 27-month absense?

(A) The U.S. Open

(B) Wimbleton

(C) The Canadian Open

(D) The Australian Open

322. Wilma Rudolph, track and field star of the 1950s and 1960s, suffered from which of the following as a child?

(A) Blindness

(B) Polio

(C) Scoliosis

(D) Bubonic plague

323. Annie Oakley became the first internationally-known female athlete by dominating which of the following?

(A) Track and field

(B) Rowing

(C) Soccer

(D) Sharpshooting

324. Which of the following is true of Shirley Muldowney?

  (A) She is the only woman to win the Indianapolis 500.

  (B) She is the only woman to be elected to the Motorsports Hall of Fame.

  (C) She is the only female athlete to have a movie made about her.

  (D) She is the only woman to ever race a dragster.

325. Who was nicknamed "Lady Magic" and was the first woman to play in a men's professional basketball league?

  (A) Nancy Lieberman-Cline

  (B) Pat Summitt

  (C) Cheryl Miller

  (D) Sheryl Swoopes

326. Olympic gymnastics star Olga Korbut was from which country?

  (A) East Germany

  (B) West Germany

  (C) USA

  (D) USSR

327. Who was the target of Tonya Harding's ex-husband's attack with a metal pipe prior to the 1994 Olympics?

  (A) Tara Lipinksi

  (B) Michelle Kwan

  (C) Nancy Kerrigan

  (D) Tonya Harding

328. Hockey debuted as an official women's Olympic sport in which year?

  (A) 1976

  (B) 1980

  (C) 1988

  (D) 1998

329. Who was the first player in WNBA history to record a triple double?

   (A)   Sheryl Swoopes

   (B)   Margo Dydek

   (C)   Sue Bird

   (D)   Jennifer Azzi

330. Who was the first woman to swim in four Olympics?

   (A)   Summer Sanders

   (B)   Brooke Bennett

   (C)   Dara Torres

   (D)   Jenny Thompson

331. Who was the Norwegian figure skater who won three Olympic gold medals and ten consecutive world championships?

   (A)   Peggy Fleming

   (B)   Sonja Henie

   (C)   Bonnie Blair

   (D)   Katarina Witt

332. What golfing great won her first amateur event at age 12 then went on to win more than 45 LPGA events, not to mention being named rookie of the year and player of the year in the same year (1978)?

   (A)   Anika Sorenstam

   (B)   Mickey Wright

   (C)   Louise Suggs

   (D)   Nancy Lopez

333. Which American woman has more individual Olympic gold medals than any other American female Olympian?

   (A)   Bonnie Blair

   (B)   Janet Evans

   (C)   Pat McCormick

   (D)   Jackie Joyner-Kersee

334. Who is the only woman to have won all four Grand Slam events at least four times?

(A) Billie Jean King

(B) Martina Navratilova

(C) Steffi Graf

(D) Chris Evert

335. Julie Krone broke the gender barrier and became one of the best in which of the following sports?

(A) Distance running

(B) Rodeo

(C) Horse racing

(D) Rowing

336. Bonnie Blair made her mark in which of the following Olympic sports?

(A) Speed skating

(B) Figure skating

(C) Cross-country skiing

(D) Downhill skiing

337. Mary Decker-Slaney, a world-class distance runner, is best remembered for which of the following moments in her career?

(A) Setting a world record in the mile at the age of 12

(B) Setting a world record in the mile at the age of 37

(C) Setting a world record in the marathon at the age of 12

(D) Being accidentally tripped by Zola Budd in the 3,000 meter race at the 1984 Olympics

338. Picabo Street was the premier women's athlete in which of the following sports during the 1990s?

(A) Synchronized swimming

(B) Downhill skiing

(C) Figure skating

(D) Powerlifting

339. Which of the following women has been an eight-time world champion triathlete?

(A) Marion Jones

(B) Mary Decker-Slaney

(C) Paula Newby-Fraser

(D) Jackie Joyner-Kersee

340. When was the first time the Indy 500 had two women in the starting field?

(A) 2002

(B) 2001

(C) 2000

(D) 1999

341. Dorothy Kamenshek's claim to fame is which of the following?

(A) She is considered the greatest women's professional baseball player of all-time.

(B) She won more volleyball championships in her career than anyone else.

(C) She won more Boston Marathon's than any other racer, man or woman.

(D) She was the first woman to play professional football.

342. Who is the nation's all-time leading scorer in women's hockey and only the second woman to ever broadcast an NHL game?

(A) Manon Rheaume

(B) Cammi Granato

(C) Carisa Zaban

(D) Sara Decosta

343. Lyn St. James made her mark in which branch of auto racing?

(A) Drag racing

(B) Funny car racing

(C) Monster truck racing

(D) Indy car racing

344. Flo Hyman, who stood 6'5" tall, became the greatest U.S. woman's player of which sport?

(A) Basketball

(B) Water polo

(C) Lacrosse

(D) Volleyball

345. What Eastern Bloc figure skater went from two-time Olympic champion to sex symbol in the 1980s and 1990s?

(A) Sonja Henie

(B) Katarina Witt

(C) Tara Lapinski

(D) Tai Babilonia

346. Tennis Hall of Famer Evonne Goolagong was born in and grew up in which of the following countries?

(A) Australia

(B) New Zealand

(C) Argentina

(D) Bulgaria

347. Which softball pitcher has won an NCAA championship at UCLA, a world championship, and an Olympic championship?

(A) Dot Richardson

(B) Nancy Evans

(C) Lisa Fernandez

(D) Julie Marshall

348. Pat McCormick won Olympic gold in which two events?

(A) Springboard diving and platform diving

(B) Springboard diving and cliff diving

(C) Platform diving and cliff diving

(D) Synchronized swimming and platform diving

349. Which track and field star won two bronze, one silver, and three gold medals over the course of four consecutive Olympics and was named as *Sports Illustrated For Women*'s Greatest Female Athlete of the Twentieth Century?

(A) Jackie Joyner-Kersee

(B) Marion Jones

(C) Florence Griffith Joyner

(D) Wilma Rudolph

350. How tall was Old Dominion basketball star Anne Donovan who averaged 20 points and 14.5 rebounds per game during her career?

(A) 5′0″

(B) 5′8″

(C) 6′2″

(D) 6′8″

351. Chinese diver Fu Minxia can claim which of the following as a career accomplishment?

(A) Being the youngest person to ever win an Olympic medal

(B) Being the youngest woman to ever win an Olympic medal

(C) Being the youngest world champion in any aquatic event at the age of 12

(D) Being the only Chinese diver to compete in the Olympics

352. Who was the youngest player on the 1991 World Championship-winning U.S. women's soccer team?

(A) Mia Hamm

(B) Brandi Chastain

(C) Julie Foudy

(D) Briana Scurry

353. Which great tennis player helped break the color barrier in professional tennis?

(A) Evonne Goolagong

(B) Alice Marble

(C) Maureen Connolly

(D) Althea Gibson

354. What two-sport star played professionally in both tennis and golf?

(A) Althea Gibson

(B) Babe Didrikson Zaharias

(C) Connie Carpenter

(D) Sheila Young

355. The Williams sisters, who have dominated tennis the last several years, are which of the following?

(A) Venus and Seraphim

(B) Serena and Venus

(C) Madonna and Serena

(D) Seraphim and Vicki

356. After what sporting event did Brandi Chastain slide on her knees and pull off her jersey making her an instant celebrity?

(A) 1999 WNBA championship game

(B) 1999 World Cheerleading championship

(C) 1999 World Cup championship game

(D) 1999 Wimbledon championship game

357. Who was the second African American woman to play in a Grand Slam final?

(A) Althea Gibson

(B) Zina Garrison

(C) Serena Williams

(D) Venus William

CHAPTER 7 ANSWERS

307. **The correct answer is (B).** In 1984, Mary Lou Retton won the gold medal for All-Around. She also won the silver medal in the Vault and the bronze in the Uneven Bars and Floor Exercise.

308. **The correct answer is (C).** Billie Jean King also defeated Bobby Riggs in the infamous "Battle of the Sexes" grudge match in 1973.

309. **The correct answer is (A).** Mia Hamm became an international superstar after scoring more goals than any other woman in Division I NCAA women's soccer history.

310. **The correct answer is (D).** "Babe" Didrikson Zaharias may be the greatest and most dominant female athlete of all-time.

311. **The correct answer is (C).** Nadia Comaneci finished the Olympics that year with three golds, one silver, and one bronze to go along with the seven perfect 10s she scored in the process.

312. **The correct answer is (D).** Affectionately known as "Flo-Jo," Florence Griffith Joyner was and still is considered the world's fastest woman even after her death in 1998.

313. **The correct answer is (D).** On August 30, 2001, Ashley Martin kicked an extra-point for Jacksonville State (Alabama) and became the first woman to ever score in a Division I football game.

314. **The correct answer is (B).** Even though she was drafted at the age of 15 by a professional softball team, Dot's goal was to play for the U.S. Olympic team and win the gold, which she did.

315. **The correct answer is (C).** In 1972, Title IX was passed. This legislation said that financial assistance based on athletics must be distributed proportionately between men's and women's athletics, effectively requiring the addition of many women's programs to major universities.

316. **The correct answer is (D).** An LPGA player may enter the LPGA Hall of Fame with 40 wins (none of them being a major), 35 wins plus a major, or 30 wins plus two different majors.

317. **The correct answer is (A).** Gertrude Ederle became the first woman to swim the English Channel, and she broke the current men's record time while doing it.

318. **The correct answer is (D).** Susan Butcher, one of the best dog-sled mushers in the world, has won the Iditarod more than any other man or woman.

319. **The correct answer is (B).** Christy Martin, one of today's premier women's boxers, was the first woman to ever be featured on Pay-Per-View.

320. **The correct answer is (C).** Navratilova, the native of Prague, won 18 Grand Slam singles titles and 31 Grand Slam doubles titles in her run of 168 singles and 165 doubles titles.

321. **The correct answer is (C).** Seles won the first tournament she played in after returning to tennis from a 27-month absence. She reached the finals of the U.S. Open two weeks later.

322. **The correct answer is (B).** Wilma Rudolph, stricken with polio as a child, could not even walk yet she went on to become the first American woman to capture three Olympic gold medals.

323. **The correct answer is (D).** Annie Oakley won international fame with her amazing sharpshooting and feats of marksmanship in the late nineteenth and early twentieth centuries.

324. **The correct answer is (B).** Muldowney has been one of drag racing's greatest stars and is currently the only woman in the Motorsports Hall of Fame.

325. **The correct answer is (A).** Nancy Lieberman-Cline became the first woman to play in a men's professional basketball league when she joined Springfield Fame in 1986.

326. The correct answer is (D). Olga Korbut was born in Belarus, a part of the former USSR.

327. The correct answer is (C). Tonya Harding's ex attacked Nancy Kerrigan and hit her leg with a pipe as she was leaving a practice arena; Kerrigan was later named to the Olympic team.

328. The correct answer is (D). The USA won the first Women's Hockey Olympic gold medal in Nagano in 1998.

329. The correct answer is (A). In 1999, Sheryl Swoopes recorded the WNBA's first triple double with 14 points, 15 rebounds, and 10 assists.

330. The correct answer is (C). Dara Torres swam for the United States in 1984, 1988, 1992, and 2000.

331. The correct answer is (B). Norwegian skating superstar Sonja Henie competed in her first Olympics at age 11; the rest, as they say, is history.

332. The correct answer is (D). Nancy Lopez put women's golf on the map in the 1980s and remains one of golf's greatest stars today.

333. The correct answer is (A). Bonnie Blair won five gold medals over the course of three different Olympiads.

334. The correct answer is (C). Steffi Graf is also the only player to win all four Grand Slam events and an Olympic medal in the same calendar year.

335. The correct answer is (C). Julie Krone is the only female (horse racing) jockey to ever win a Triple Crown race, the Breeder's Cup in 1993.

336. The correct answer is (A). Bonnie Blair won gold medals in 1988, 1992, and 1994 in speed skating, and she is widely regarded as the best female speed skater of all time.

337. The correct answer is (D). After Zola Budd tripped Mary Decker-Slaney in the 3000 meter race in the 1984 Olympics, a race in which Decker-Slaney was the hands-down favorite, Decker-Slaney got up and went straight to the showers.

338. The correct answer is (B). Picabo Street won a national championship and several Olympic medals in downhill skiing.

339. The correct answer is (C). Paula Newby-Fraser has won more than 20 career Ironman races and has been world champion eight times.

340. The correct answer is (B). In 2001, 19-year-old Sarah Fisher was in her first Indy 500, while Lyn St. James, the oldest competitor, was in her final Indy 500.

341. The correct answer is (A). Dorothy Kamenshek played for the Rockford Peaches from 1943–1951 where she won two batting titles and made seven All-Star appearances for the All-American Girls Baseball League.

342. The correct answer is (B). Cammi Granato is the all-time scoring leader in U.S. women's hockey history and has played with U.S. women's hockey since it was born in 1990.

343. The correct answer is (D). Lyn St. James was only the second woman to ever qualify for the Indy 500 and was named Rookie of the Year in 1992. She is currently a racer-owner.

344. The correct answer is (D). Flo Hyman helped put the U.S. women's volleyball program on the map during the 1970s and 1980s.

345. The correct answer is (B). Katarina Witt made the transition from champion skater to media darling and sex symbol, a transition not easily made by a skater from the Eastern Bloc.

346. The correct answer is (A). Evonne Goolagong was born in and grew up in Barrellan, Australia, and is actually of Aboriginal descent.

347. The correct answer is (C). Lisa Fernandez has accomplished practically everything there is to accomplish in fast-pitch softball, including NCAA, world, and Olympic championships.

348. The correct answer is (A). In a feat matched only by Greg Louganis, Pat McCormick won Olympic gold in both platform and springboard diving.

349. The correct answer is (A). Jackie Joyner-Kersee may very well be the greatest female track and field athlete of all-time.

350. The correct answer is (D). Anne Donovan towered over nearly everyone, including teammate Nancy Lieberman-Cline, at 6'8".

351. The correct answer is (C). Fu Mingxia won a world championship in diving at the age of 12, thereby making her the youngest to ever do so; Fu Mingxia didn't know how to swim when she first began diving only a few years earlier.

352. The correct answer is (A). Mia Hamm, at age 19, was the youngest player on the 1991 World Championship-winning U.S. team.

353. The correct answer is (D). Althea Gibson helped break the color barrier in tennis while at the same time winning nearly 100 titles, including 5 Grand Slam titles.

354. The correct answer is (A). Althea Gibson also played professional golf and helped break the color barrier there just as she had in tennis.

355. The correct answer is (B). Venus and Serena Williams are poised to be the most successful sister-sister combination to ever play professional sports if they continue to dominate the tennis world the way they have for the last years.

356. The correct answer is (C). Brandi Chastain kicked the World Cup championship-clinching penalty kick for the U.S.A. in 1999 and exuberantly took off her jersey in celebration.

357. The correct answer is (B). In 1990, Zina Garrison lost to Martina Navratilova in the Wimbledon final. Navratilova won her ninth and final Wimbledon title.

CHAPTER 8

In the Bunker:
Golf

358. What is the real name of Tiger Woods?

   (A)   Tiger Woods

   (B)   Elwood Woods

   (C)   Eldrick Woods

   (D)   Eldridge Woods

359. A golf shot that is hit over the top and then bounces around erratically is known as a

   (A)   wild one.

   (B)   rabbit.

   (C)   worm burner.

   (D)   hip hop.

> The more I practice, the luckier I get.
> —GARY PLAYER

360. What LPGA player holds the record for most tournaments won with 88?

(A) Nancy Lopez

(B) Karrie Webb

(C) Dinah Shore

(D) Kathy Whitworth

361. Who was the oldest player to win a tournament on the PGA tour?

(A) Arnold Palmer

(B) Jack Nicklaus

(C) Chi Chi Rodriguez

(D) Sam Snead

362. Who was the youngest player to win a tournament on the PGA tour?

(A) Johnny McDermott

(B) Tiger Woods

(C) Phil Mickelson

(D) Byron Nelson

363. Which U.S. major is open to both amateurs and professionals?

(A) The U.S. Amateur

(B) The U.S. Open

(C) The Masters

(D) The Skins Game

364. Who was the first golfer to earn $1 million from playing golf?

(A) Byron Nelson

(B) Arnold Palmer

(C) Curtis Strange

(D) Ben Hogan

365. What famous author once said, "Golf is a good walk spoiled"?

(A) William Faulkner

(B) William Shakespeare

(C) Winston Churchill

(D) Mark Twain

366. The first golf balls were made of what?

(A) Leather stuffed with cotton

(B) Leather stuffed with straw

(C) Leather stuffed with wool

(D) Leather stuffed with feathers

367. What feature was added to golf balls to make them fly farther and more accurately?

(A) Dimples

(B) A white, polished surface

(C) A cork core

(D) A graphite core

368. What legendary golfer went 113 consecutive events without missing the cut?

(A) Ben Hogan

(B) Tiger Woods

(C) Byron Nelson

(D) Bobby Jones

369. What LPGA player holds the 18-hole scoring record with a blistering 59?

(A) Annika Sorenstam

(B) Beth Daniel

(C) Karrie Webb

(D) Se Ri Pak

370. How old was the youngest player, Scott Statler in 1962, to shoot a hole-in-one?

    (A) 4 years old

    (B) 5 years old

    (C) 9 years old

    (D) 11 years old

371. Because of her superstitious nature, what will Nancy Lopez never use in a golf tournament?

    (A) A scuffed ball

    (B) A tee that someone else discarded

    (C) Shoes she wore in a tournament that she didn't win

    (D) A hat with sweat stains

372. What LPGA great holds the record for the most career holes-in-one?

    (A) Babe Didrikson Zaharias

    (B) Annika Sorenstam

    (C) Nancy Lopez

    (D) Kathy Whitworth

373. What PGA player holds the record for the lowest scoring average for a season?

    (A) Ben Hogan

    (B) Curtis Strange

    (C) Mark O'Meara

    (D) Tiger Woods

374. How many career wins does Sam Snead have?

    (A) 51

    (B) 61

    (C) 71

    (D) 81

375. What two players won at least one tournament for seventeen consecutive years?

  (A) Jack Nicklaus and Arnold Palmer

  (B) Bobby Jones and Byron Nelson

  (C) Sam Snead and Arnold Palmer

  (D) Bobby Jones and Jack Nicklaus

376. In 1999, Maria Hjorth shot how many birdies to set the single-season record?

  (A) 1,002

  (B) 408

  (C) 333

  (D) 220

377. The grass that borders the green is known as "the fringe" or what other name?

  (A) Buzz cut

  (B) Collar

  (C) Frog hair

  (D) Leather

378. In which country was golf invented?

  (A) England

  (B) Wales

  (C) Ireland

  (D) Scotland

379. Who was the youngest tournament winner in LPGA history?

  (A) Marlene Hagge

  (B) Se Ri Pak

  (C) Karrie Webb

  (D) Nancy Lopez

380. Who holds the record for most earning in a calendar year with $9,188,321?

(A) Ernie Els

(B) Tiger Woods

(C) Justin Leonard

(D) John Daly

381. Which player has spent the most years on the Top 10 Money List?

(A) Byron Nelson

(B) Walter Hagen

(C) Jack Nicklaus

(D) Sam Snead

382. Who won the U.S. Open just months after a terrible car accident threatened his career?

(A) Ben Hogan

(B) Arnold Palmer

(C) Fuzzy Zoeller

(D) Lee Trevino

383. What color is the jacket that the Masters winner receives?

(A) Red

(B) Yellow

(C) Blue

(D) Green

384. What is a banana ball?

(A) A yellow golf ball

(B) A badly hooked ball

(C) A badly sliced ball

(D) A ball whose covering is peeling off

385. Jack Nicklaus always plays with three of what in his pocket?

(A) Three balls and three tees

(B) Three tees and three pennies

(C) Three pennies and three quarters

(D) Three dollar bills and three Susan B. Anthony dollars

386. Which LPGA player holds the records for most money won in a rookie year and for most money won in a calendar year (each record is from a different year)?

(A) Karrie Webb

(B) Se Ri Pak

(C) Beth Daniel

(D) Annika Sorenstam

387. What is the maximum number of clubs that can be carried in a golf bag during a round?

(A) 16

(B) 15

(C) 14

(D) 13

388. Which of the following was first used in the game of golf in 1922?

(A) A wooden tee

(B) A dimpled golf ball

(C) A sand wedge

(D) A pitching wedge

389. What is the proper depth of a golf hole?

(A) Not more than 8 inches deep

(B) Not more than 7 inches deep

(C) Not more than 6 inches deep

(D) Not more than 4 inches deep

390. Who is the only woman to win the same event four years in a row?

   (A) Nancy Lopez

   (B) Laura Davies

   (C) Mickey Wright

   (D) Juli Inkster

391. Which of the following is *not* included in the Grand Slam of Golf?

   (A) The U.S. Open

   (B) The British Open

   (C) The French Open

   (D) The Masters

392. What player has played in the most Ryder Cup matches in history?

   (A) Arnold Palmer

   (B) Lenny Wadkins

   (C) Bernhard Langer

   (D) Nick Faldo

393. Greg Norman is often referred to by which of the following nicknames?

   (A) "The Aussie"

   (B) "The Shark"

   (C) "The Barracuda"

   (D) "The Piranha"

394. Who was the first golfer to market golf equipment with his name on it?

   (A) Arnold Palmer

   (B) Byron Nelson

   (C) Walter Hagen

   (D) Jack Nicklaus

395. Who shot an amazing 19 consecutive sub-70 rounds over a span in which he won 19 tournaments and 11 tournaments in a row?

(A) Tiger Woods

(B) Sam Snead

(C) Mark Calcavecchia

(D) Byron Nelson

396. Which of the following golfers has never been a wire-to-wire winner of the Masters?

(A) Craig Wood

(B) Arnold Palmer

(C) Tom Watson

(D) Jack Nicklaus

397. Who is the only honorary member of the LPGA Hall of Fame?

(A) Betsy King

(B) Amy Alcott

(C) Patty Sheehan

(D) Dinah Shore

398. Who is the youngest player to ever play in the Ryder Cup?

(A) Sergio Garcia

(B) Tiger Woods

(C) Jose Maria Olazabal

(D) Jack Burke

399. Who served as the first president of the LPGA?

(A) Patty Berg

(B) Mickey Wright

(C) Babe Didrikson Zaharias

(D) Louise Suggs

400. Which of the following players has a bridge named after him at Augusta?

(A)   Gene Sarazen

(B)   Tiger Woods

(C)   Payne Stewart

(D)   Paul Azinger

401. What is golf slang for a ball buried in the sand?

(A)   A gopher ball

(B)   Buried treasure

(C)   A fried egg

(D)   An ostrich head

402. A double eagle, or three under par for a single hole, is sometimes called which of the following?

(A)   A sea gull

(B)   An albatross

(C)   A monkey

(D)   A bald eagle

403. Who, in 1754, laid out the famous "Thirteen Basic Rules of Golf"?

(A)   The Society of St. Andrews Golfers

(B)   The PGA

(C)   The LPGA

(D)   King George II

404. Which LPGA star scored the lowest scoring average for one season with 69.43?

(A)   Annika Sorenstam

(B)   Laura Davies

(C)   Lorie Kane

(D)   Karrie Webb

405. Which PGA rookie set the record for most money won by a rookie with $1,864,584?

(A) Tiger Woods

(B) Sergio Garcia

(C) Carlos Franco

(D) David Duval

406. Who holds the record for most consecutive victories and for most victories in a calendar year?

(A) Sam Snead

(B) Arnold Palmer

(C) Tiger Woods

(D) Byron Nelson

407. Why was golf once banned in Scotland by King James II?

(A) A golf ball broke a window in his castle.

(B) Golf was interfering with the military training of his soldiers.

(C) The green fees became too expensive and interfered with the collection of taxes.

(D) The English defeated the Scottish in an international competition.

408. Among all golfers with 25 or more rounds played in the Masters, who holds the tournament record for best career scoring average?

(A) Phil Mickelson

(B) Greg Norman

(C) Tiger Woods

(D) Nick Faldo

409. Who was the first five-time winner of the Masters?

(A) Ben Hogan

(B) Sam Snead

(C) Raymond Floyd

(D) Jack Nicklaus

CHAPTER 8 ANSWERS

358. **The correct answer is (C).** Tiger's real name is Eldrick; Tiger is just a nickname given to him by his father.

359. **The correct answer is (B).** A golf shot that is topped and then bounces erratically is often called a rabbit and is occasionally called a screamer or a scooter.

360. **The correct answer is (D).** Kathy Whitworth won an incredible 88 tournaments in her career.

361. **The correct answer is (D).** Sam Snead won the Greater Greensboro Open in 1965 at the age of 52 years and 10 months.

362. **The correct answer is (A).** Johnny McDermott won the 1911 U.S. Open at the tender age of 19 years and 10 months.

363. **The correct answer is (B).** The U.S. Open is open to both amateur and professional golfers.

364. **The correct answer is (C).** Curtis Strange won $1,147,644 in 1988.

365. **The correct answer is (D).** The quote illustrates the uncanny wit of Mark Twain.

366. **The correct answer is (D).** The first true golf balls were actually made of leather coverings stuffed with feathers.

367. **The correct answer is (A).** Dimples were added to the surface of the golf ball to make them more accurate and to help them travel farther.

368. **The correct answer is (C).** Byron Nelson went 113 consecutive events without missing a cut during the 1940s.

369. **The correct answer is (A).** Annika Sorenstam shot a 59 in the second round of the 2001 Standard Register Ping.

370. The correct answer is (A). Scott Statler in Greensburg, Pennsylvania, shot a hole-in-one when he was 4 years old.

371. The correct answer is (B). Nancy Lopez will not use a tee that someone else has discarded.

372. The correct answer is (D). Kathy Whitworth registered an amazing eleven career holes-in-one.

373. The correct answer is (D). Tiger Woods averaged 67.79 for the entire 2000 season and holds the record for lowest scoring average over a season.

374. The correct answer is (D). Sam Snead has won 81 career tournaments and holds the record for most career wins.

375. The correct answer is (A). Jack Nicklaus, from 1962 to 1978, and Arnold Palmer, from 1955 to 1971, each went seventeen consecutive years with at least one win.

376. The correct answer is (B). Maria Hjorth shot an incredible 408 birdies in 1999 to set the single-season record.

377. The correct answer is (C). As strange as it may be, the fringe is also known as frog hair.

378. The correct answer is (D). Golf was invented in Scotland about 1,000 years ago.

379. The correct answer is (A). Marlene Hagge won the 1952 Sarasota Open at the age of 18 years and 14 days.

380. The correct answer is (B). In 2000, Tiger Woods won more than $9 million on tour alone.

381. The correct answer is (C). Jack Nicklaus spent 18 years among the top ten money winners in golf.

382. The correct answer is (A). Ben Hogan won the U.S. Open just months after he broke a collarbone, an ankle, and the pelvis in a car accident.

383. The correct answer is (D). The winner of the Masters receives a green jacket.

384. The correct answer is (C). A banana ball is a badly sliced ball whose flight resembles a banana shape.

385. The correct answer is (B). Because of a superstition, Jack Nicklaus always plays with three tees and three pennies in his pocket.

386. The correct answer is (D). Annika Sorenstam won $1,002,000 in her rookie year, 1996, and won $1,876,853 in 2000.

387. The correct answer is (C). A golfer may carry only 14 clubs in a bag during a round of golf, although a damaged club may be replaced during a round.

388. The correct answer is (A). Until 1922, golfers made a small mound of sand or dirt from which to hit the ball.

389. The correct answer is (D). In 1894, the Royal and Ancient decreed that a golf hole shall be 4 1/4 inches wide and no more than four inches deep.

390. The correct answer is (B). Laura Davies won the Standard Register PING tournament from 1994 to 1997.

391. The correct answer is (C). The French Open is not included in the Grand Slam of Golf.

392. The correct answer is (D). Nick Faldo has played in a record 11 matches between 1977 and 1997.

393. The correct answer is (B). Greg Norman, an Australian, is often called by his nickname, "the Shark."

394. The correct answer is (C). Walter Hagen was the first golfer to have his name on golf equipment.

395. The correct answer is (D). Byron Nelson accomplished this amazing feat in 1945.

396. The correct answer is (C). Craig Wood went wire-to-wire in 1941, Arnold Palmer in 1960, and Jack Nicklaus in 1972.

397. The correct answer is (D). Dinah Shore became an honorary member of the LPGA Hall of Fame in 1994.

398. The correct answer is (A). Sergio Garcia played in the Ryder Cup in 1999 at the age of 19 years, 8 months, 15 days.

399. The correct answer is (A). Patty Berg was the LPGA's first president.

400. The correct answer is (A). Gene Sarazen actually has a bridge named after him at the famed Augusta National course.

401. The correct answer is (C). A ball buried in the sand is called a fried egg or a plugged lie.

402. The correct answer is (B). A double eagle is sometimes referred to as an albatross.

403. The correct answer is (A). The Scottish group known as the Society of St. Andrews Golfers laid out the original "Thirteen Basic Rules of Golf."

404. The correct answer is (D). Karrie Webb averaged 69.43 for the entire season in 1999.

405. The correct answer is (C). Carlos Franco earned a record amount of money on the tour in 1999.

406. The correct answer is (D). Byron Nelson won 11 consecutive tournaments and 18 total tournaments in 1945.

407. The correct answer is (B). King James II of Scotland banned "golf" because golf games were interfering with the training of soldiers for wars against England.

408. The correct answer is (A). Phil Mickelson holds the record for best career scoring average.

409. The correct answer is (D). Jack Nicklaus won the Masters six times total—the first time in 1963 and the last in 1986. No one else has won more than four Masters championships.

CHAPTER 9

Serve and Volley:
Tennis

410. Wimbledon is played on which of the following surfaces?

(A) Clay

(B) Hard court

(C) Grass

(D) Astroturf

411. What name is given to a serve that is touched by the opponent but not returned in play?

(A) An ace

(B) A service winner

(C) A carry

(D) A let

A perfect combination of violent action taking place in an atmosphere of total tranquility.
—BILLIE JEAN KING

412. Who is the first man to win Wimbledon five straight times?

(A) Jimmy Connors

(B) Boris Becker

(C) Ivan Lendl

(D) Bjorn Borg

413. Which of the following is *not* part of the Grand Slam of tennis?

(A) European Open

(B) Australian Open

(C) French Open

(D) U.S. Open

414. What was the final result of the Battle of the Sexes in 1973 featuring Billie Jean King and male chauvinist Bobby Riggs?

(A) King defeated Riggs.

(B) Riggs defeated King.

(C) The match was called early because of bad weather.

(D) The match was called because Riggs had chest pains.

415. Who is the only player to win at least one Grand Slam event every year for thirteen consecutive years?

(A) Martina Navratilova

(B) Tracy Austin

(C) Venus Williams

(D) Chris Evert

416. Cyclops refers to which of the following?

(A) A player who wears a headband

(B) A mechanical device that shoots tennis balls

(C) A mechanical device that checks the service line on serves

(D) The judge behind the service line

417. Which of the following is the international tennis tournament that matches country against country?

(A) The Ryder Cup

(B) The Grey Cup

(C) The Stanley Cup

(D) The Davis Cup

418. Who is the first unseeded player to win Wimbledon?

(A) Pete Sampras

(B) Andre Agassi

(C) Don Budge

(D) Boris Becker

419. Who was the first person ever disqualified from a Grand Slam event for bad behavior?

(A) Billie Jean King

(B) John McEnroe

(C) Steffi Graf

(D) Jimmy Connors

420. Who was the first woman to ever win the Grand Slam?

(A) Maureen Connolly

(B) Margaret Court Smith

(C) Steffi Graf

(D) Venus Williams

421. "Love" in tennis, meaning zero score, originally came from a French word (*l'oeuf*) meaning what?

(A) Zero

(B) Mercy

(C) Without

(D) Egg

422. Who was the first black woman to win Wimbledon?

   (A)   Althea Gibson

   (B)   Evonne Goolagong

   (C)   Venus Williams

   (D)   Serena Williams

423. Which of the following scores is referred to as "deuce"?

   (A)   15–0

   (B)   15–15

   (C)   30–30

   (D)   40–40

424. How long was the longest tennis match ever played?

   (A)   44 games

   (B)   99 games

   (C)   126 games

   (D)   147 games

425. Who is the only man to ever win the U.S. Open on three different surfaces?

   (A)   John McEnroe

   (B)   Jimmy Connors

   (C)   Michael Chang

   (D)   Ivan Lendl

426. What is a Saba-tweeny?

   (A)   A chair placed between courts for players to use between matches

   (B)   A restroom break between matches

   (C)   A between-the-legs shot made famous by Gabriela Sabatini

   (D)   A special racket made from all synthetic materials

427. Where is the International Tennis Hall of Fame, formerly known as the National Tennis Hall of Fame?

(A) Canton, Ohio

(B) Cooperstown, New York

(C) Newport, Rhode Island

(D) Springfield, Massachusetts

428. Who is the last left-handed player to win the U.S. Open?

(A) Manuel Orantes

(B) Jimmy Connors

(C) Arthur Ashe

(D) John McEnroe

429. Who is the youngest men's player ever to win the French Open?

(A) Pete Sampras

(B) Michael Chang

(C) Boris Becker

(D) Don Budge

430. Who became the first female athlete to win more than $100,000 in prize money in a year?

(A) Martina Navratilova

(B) Martina Hingis

(C) Billie Jean King

(D) Tracy Austin

431. The French Open is held annually at Roland Garros in which of the following cities?

(A) Paris

(B) Lyons

(C) Marseilles

(D) Cannes

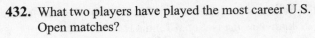

432. What two players have played the most career U.S. Open matches?

   (A) Chris Evert and John McEnroe

   (B) Tracy Austin and Jimmy Connors

   (C) Boris Becker and Chris Evert

   (D) Chris Evert and Jimmy Connors

433. The women's version of the Davis Cup is known as which of the following?

   (A) Women's Davis Cup

   (B) Federation Cup

   (C) Stanley Cup

   (D) Ryder Cup

434. What three colors are legal for balls in most tennis tournaments?

   (A) White, yellow, and green

   (B) White, green, and orange

   (C) Green, orange, and yellow

   (D) White, orange, and yellow

435. How old was the oldest Wimbledon men's singles winner, A.W. Gore, when he won the championship in 1909?

   (A) 64 years old

   (B) 52 years old

   (C) 41 years old

   (D) 36 years old

436. A regulation tennis net is 3 feet high at the center of the net. How high is the net at each end?

   (A) 2' 6"

   (B) 3' 0"

   (C) 3' 6"

   (D) 4' 0"

437. Which of the following is a Wimbledon tradition?

   (A) Strawberries and cream

   (B) Peaches and cream

   (C) Cookies and cream

   (D) Milk and honey

438. How many Grand Slam titles did Martina Navratilova win amongst her 167 total event wins?

   (A) 9

   (B) 11

   (C) 18

   (D) 47

439. In which city is the Australian Open held each year?

   (A) Melbourne

   (B) Sydney

   (C) Brisbane

   (D) Perth

440. What player went years without playing at Wimbledon because he refused to follow Wimbledon's "almost entirely white" dress code for players?

   (A) Boris Becker

   (B) Andre Agassi

   (C) Michael Chang

   (D) Pat Cash

441. Which player has made the most Challenge or Final Round appearances in Davis Cup history?

   (A) Bill Tilden

   (B) Jimmy Connors

   (C) Ivan Lendl

   (D) Perry Jones

442. Which country has won the most Federation Cup titles?

(A) Spain

(B) USA

(C) Australia

(D) Czechoslovakia

443. What tennis legend is remembered as much for his humanitarian work as for his tennis accomplishments?

(A) Don Budge

(B) Arthur Ashe

(C) Marcelo Rios

(D) Bill Tilden

444. What was the term used for the now-illegal double strung tennis rackets made popular in the 1970s?

(A) Double barrel rackets

(B) Pipe rackets

(C) Spaghetti rackets

(D) Cat gut rackets

445. The WTA Tour Championship formerly went by which of the following names?

(A) Carolina Tennis Tour

(B) Women's Professional Tennis Championship

(C) Minnesota Fats Championship

(D) Virginia Slims Championship

446. In all official matters at Wimbledon, which of the following words are used instead of "men's and women's"?

(A) "Gents' and lassies'"

(B) "Gentlemen's and ladies'"

(C) "Lads' and lassies'"

(D) "Lords' and ladies'"

447. On what surface do players play at the French Open?

   (A) Grass

   (B) Hard court

   (C) Clay

   (D) Astroturf

448. Some tennis courts in India are made from what unusual substance?

   (A) Charcoal

   (B) Corn husks

   (C) Recycled automobile tires

   (D) Cow dung

449. Which country has the most men's and women's singles titles at Wimbledon?

   (A) USA

   (B) Great Britain

   (C) France

   (D) Australia

450. Which of the following countries has never had a representative win a men's singles title at Wimbledon?

   (A) Croatia

   (B) Spain

   (C) Egypt

   (D) South Africa

451. In which of the following ways can a player hit a winner without hitting the ball over the net?

   (A) The ball can go through the net.

   (B) The ball can go under the net.

   (C) The ball can go around the net post and into the opponent's court.

   (D) The ball can hit the opponent at the net and ricochet out.

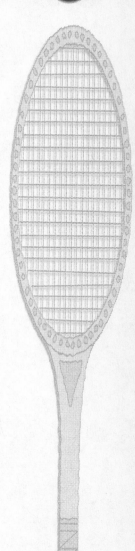

452. Bjorn Borg practiced what superstitious ritual whenever he participated at Wimbledon?

(A) He refused to shave.

(B) He refused to bathe.

(C) He wore the same clothes each day.

(D) He ate only steamed rice three times daily.

453. Who is the only player to ever win the Grand Slam in both singles and doubles competition?

(A) John McEnroe

(B) Margaret Court Smith

(C) Rod Laver

(D) Ken Fletcher

454. What alteration to Gertrude Moran's tennis attire caused a major controversy at Wimbledon in 1949?

(A) The addition of a pink stripe on her blouse

(B) The addition of lace to her panties

(C) The raising of her skirt above her ankles

(D) The removal of her sleeves

455. Which female star was seeded first a record nine times at the U.S. Open?

(A) Martina Navratilova

(B) Martina Hingis

(C) Steffi Graf

(D) Venus Williams

456. Until 1974, the U.S. Open was played on what surface?

(A) Grass

(B) Hard court

(C) Clay

(D) Carpet

457. What strange and traumatic event happened to Monica Seles at a tournament in Hamburg in 1993?

(A) She was attacked and stabbed.

(B) She was struck in the face with a 99 mile per hour serve.

(C) Her foot was run over by a delivery truck.

(D) She had to parachute from a crashing jet.

458. Which of the following is Renee Richards' unusual claim to fame?

(A) She plays professional tennis with only one arm.

(B) Every shot she takes, including her serve, is a backhand.

(C) She was once a man.

(D) She was the personal tennis instructor for five different U.S. presidents.

459. Who is the only Australian aboriginal to become an international tennis star?

(A) Arantxa Sanchez-Vicario

(B) Arthur Ashe

(C) Don Budge

(D) Evonne Goolagong

460. Since the inception of the ranking system in 1973, how many women have held the number one rank during the years 1973 through 2001?

(A) 7

(B) 9

(C) 12

(D) 15

461. Which one of these players won her first and last titles at Grand Slam tournaments?

(A) Chris Evert

(B) Tracy Austin

(C) Evonne Goolagong

(D) Martina Narratilova

CHAPTER 9 ANSWERS

410. The correct answer is (C). Wimbledon is played on grass courts.

411. The correct answer is (B). A service winner is a serve that is touched but not returned, while an ace is a serve that is neither touched nor returned.

412. The correct answer is (D). Between the ages of 21 and 26, Borg won Wimbledon five straight times in addition to six French Opens.

413. The correct answer is (A). Only Wimbledon and the U.S., French, and Australian Opens are part of the Grand Slam of tennis.

414. The correct answer is (A). Billie Jean King defeated Bobby Riggs in three straight sets and collected $100,000 in prize money.

415. The correct answer is (D). Chris Evert won at least one Grand Slam title every year between 1974 and 1986.

416. The correct answer is (C). Cyclops is a computerized system that uses a laser beam to check the service line on serves.

417. The correct answer is (D). The Davis Cup, named for its founder Dwight Davis, involves sixteen nations in a series of singles and doubles matches.

418. The correct answer is (D). Boris Becker won the 1985 Wimbledon as an unseeded 17-year old.

419. The correct answer is (B). In 1990, John McEnroe was disqualified from the Australian Open for verbally abusing the officials and for using obscenities.

420. The correct answer is (B). Margaret Court Smith won the Grand Slam in 1953 and became the first woman to ever do so.

421. The correct answer is (D). *L'oeuf* means egg and zero resembles an egg, thus the word love.

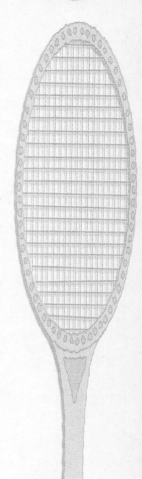

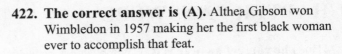
422. The correct answer is (A). Althea Gibson won Wimbledon in 1957 making her the first black woman ever to accomplish that feat.

423. The correct answer is (D). A score of 40–40 is called deuce and two straight points are needed to win the game.

424. The correct answer is (D). In 1967, Dick Leach and Tom Mozur defeated their opponents in a doubles match 3–6, 49–47, 22–20, a total of 147 games.

425. The correct answer is (B). Jimmy Connors won on grass in 1974, clay in 1976, and hard court in 1978, 1982, and in 1983.

426. The correct answer is (C). Gabriela Sabatini sometimes used a between-the-legs shot as she ran toward the baseline and the shot became known as "Saba-tweeny."

427. The correct answer is (C). The International Tennis Hall of Fame is located in Newport Casino, Newport, Rhode Island.

428. The correct answer is (D). The left-handed John McEnroe won it in 1984.

429. The correct answer is (B). Michael Chang became the youngest ever to win the French Open in 1989.

430. The correct answer is (C). Billie Jean King won more than $100,000 in 1971.

431. The correct answer is (A). The French Open is held each year at Roland Garros in Paris, France.

432. The correct answer is (D). Jimmy Connors has played in a record 115 matches, and Chris Evert has played in a record 113 matches.

433. The correct answer is (B). The women's version of the Davis Cup was founded in 1963 and is known as the Federation Cup. It is named after the founding organization, the International Tennis Federation.

434. The correct answer is (D). Balls were always white until 1972, but now yellow and even orange balls are widely accepted as legal balls.

435. The correct answer is (C). Gore was 41 years, 182 days old when he won Wimbledon in 1909.

436. The correct answer is (C). A tennis net is 3' high in the center of the net and 3' 6" high at each end.

437. The correct answer is (A). Each year visitors consume about 27,000 kilos of strawberries and about 7,000 liters of cream during the Wimbledon championships.

438. The correct answer is (C). Navratilova won an incredible 18 Grand Slam titles during her stellar career.

439. The correct answer is (A). The Australian Open is held at Melbourne Park in Melbourne each year and is the first of the Grand Slam events.

440. The correct answer is (B). The flamboyant Andre Agassi refused to wear all white clothing and went several years without ever participating in the Wimbledon championships.

441. The correct answer is (A). Bill Tilden made eleven appearances in the Challenge or Final Round of the Davis Cup.

442. The correct answer is (B). The USA has won an unparalleled seventeen Federation Cup championships.

443. The correct answer is (B). Arthur Ashe, a tennis Hall-of-Famer, devoted much of his life and his tennis earnings to such causes as AIDS research before he lost his life to AIDS.

444. The correct answer is (C). The rackets were called spaghetti rackets because of the plastic tubing used to keep the strings together.

445. The correct answer is (D). The Virginia Slims Championship was later renamed the WTA Tour Championship.

446. The correct answer is (B). Men are referred to as gentlemen and women are referred to as ladies at Wimbledon.

447. The correct answer is (C). Roland Garros, home of the French Open, is famous for its clay surface.

448. The correct answer is (D). There are some tennis courts in India made from hard, packed cow dung.

449. The correct answer is (A). The USA has a total of 33 men's singles titles and 48 women's singles titles at Wimbledon.

450. The correct answer is (D). At least one player from each of the countries listed, except South Africa, has won Wimbledon at least once.

451. The correct answer is (C). The ball can actually be hit so that it curves around the net post and into play on the other side of the net.

452. The correct answer is (A). Bjorn Borg refused to shave at Wimbledon and apparently that tactic worked; Borg won five consecutive Wimbledon titles.

453. The correct answer is (B). Margaret Court Smith won the singles Grand Slam in 1970 after winning the doubles Grand Slam with Ken Fletcher in 1963.

454. The correct answer is (B). A clothing designer added one half inch of lace to Moran's panties and made front pages of newspapers worldwide with this bold and daring move.

455. The correct answer is (C). Steffi Graf was seeded number one at the U.S. Open from 1987 to 1991 and then from 1993 to 1996.

456. The correct answer is (A). The U.S. Open was originally played on grass, then on clay, and now it is played on hard court.

457. The correct answer is (A). Strangely enough, Seles was attacked and stabbed at the tournament. She survived the attack and made a successful tennis comeback.

458. The correct answer is (C). Renee Richards was actually born as Richard Raskind, a man.

459. The correct answer is (D). Evonne Goolagong was born in Barellan, Australia and is of aboriginal descent.

460. The correct answer is (B). Steffii Graf, Matrina Navratilova, Chris Evert, Martina Hingis, Monica Seles, Lindsay Davenport, Tracy Austin, Arantxa Sanchez-Vicario, and Jennifer Capriati have held the number one rank during the eighteen years from 1973 to 2001.

461. The correct answer is (C). Evonne Gollagong won the French Open and Wimbeldon back-to-back in her first Grand Slam appearances in 1971. Her last title was Wimbeldon in 1980.

CHAPTER 10

Going for the Gold:
The Olympic Games

462. The first Olympic games were held where?

(A) Ancient Rome

(B) Ancient Greece

(C) Ancient Persia

(D) Ancient India

463. The first summer Olympics since the fourth century C.E. were held when?

(A) 1492

(B) 1496

(C) 1896

(D) 1924

Start early and begin raising the bar throughout the day.
—BRUCE JENNER

464. In what year was the Winter Olympics established?

(A) 776 B.C.E

(B) 1896

(C) 1914

(D) 1924

465. What are the colors of the Olympic rings?

(A) Blue, green, red, yellow, and black

(B) Red, yellow, black, white, and blue

(C) Black, white, orange, red, and yellow

(D) Navy blue, sky blue, red, yellow, and orange

466. What first became part of the Olympic tradition in 1928 at the games in Amsterdam?

(A) The Olympic athlete's oath

(B) The Olympic torch

(C) The five rings on the Olympic flag

(D) The awarding of medals

467. Which of the following events was actually an Olympic event at one time but is no longer an Olympic event?

(A) Three legged race

(B) Horse shoe toss

(C) Poker

(D) Tug-of-war

468. Which summer Olympic games did the United States officially boycott?

(A) Paris, 1924

(B) Berlin, 1936

(C) Tokyo, 1964

(D) Moscow, 1980

469. The 1944 Winter and Summer Olympics were *not* held for which of the following reasons?

(A) World War I

(B) World War II

(C) The Olympic committee could not decide on a host.

(D) All athletes from around the world voted to hold the Olympics in 1945 instead.

470. How many Olympians have won medals in both the Summer and Winter Olympics?

(A) 0

(B) 1

(C) 3

(D) 13

471. American swimmer Mark Spitz accomplished which of the following feats?

(A) A gold, silver, and bronze medal in each of three successive Olympics

(B) World records in sixteen Olympic events

(C) Gold medals in both swimming and equestrian events

(D) Seven gold medals in seven events in 1972

472. Which nation has won the most track and field medals in the Summer Olympics?

(A) USSR

(B) Russia

(C) USA

(D) East Germany

473. Which of the following lists is the correct list of events in the pentathlon?

(A) Running, riding, swimming, fencing, shooting

(B) Running, riding, swimming, cycling, shooting

(C) Running, riding, swimming, fencing, cycling

(D) Running, riding, shooting, fencing, javelin throw

474. Who is the only person to have won both the pentathlon and decathlon?

(A) Dan O'Brien

(B) Jim Thorpe

(C) Rafer Johnson

(D) Bruce Jenner

475. The "Fosbury Flop" is a technique used in which event?

(A) Gymnastics

(B) Diving

(C) Wrestling

(D) High jump

476. Who refused to shake the hand of Jesse Owens in the 1936 Summer Olympics?

(A) Adolf Hitler

(B) Benito Mussolini

(C) General Franco

(D) Germany's Olympic chairman

477. What country actually entered a man in a women's event in order to increase that country's medal count?

(A) USSR

(B) Bulgaria

(C) Germany

(D) Romania

478. Which countries originally opposed the establishment of a separate Winter Olympics?

(A) Scandinavian countries

(B) Asian countries

(C) African countries

(D) South American countries

479. Who was involved in the "Miracle on Ice"?

    (A) The Nigerian hockey team

    (B) The U.S. and Soviet hockey teams

    (C) Brian Boitano

    (D) Tara Lipinski

480. The movie *Cool Runnings* was about which of the following Olympic teams?

    (A) The Norwegian cross-country ski team

    (B) The Canadian speed skating team

    (C) The Ukrainian figure skating team

    (D) The Jamaican bobsled team

481. When did snowboarding debut as an Olympic sport?

    (A) 1924

    (B) 1948

    (C) 1968

    (D) 1988

482. What is the only Olympic figure skating jump taken from a forward-facing position?

    (A) Axel

    (B) Loop

    (C) Lutz

    (D) Salchow

483. Who was the youngest athlete ever to win a gold medal at the Winter Olympics?

    (A) Sonja Henie

    (B) Tara Lipinski

    (C) Michelle Kwan

    (D) Peggy Fleming

484. Eddie "the Eagle" Edwards won his 15 minutes of fame by managing not to kill himself in which sport?

(A) Giant slalom

(B) Pole vault

(C) Luge

(D) Ski jumping

485. How many times has golf been listed on the official Olympic program?

(A) Never

(B) Once

(C) Twice

(D) Three times

486. The Summer Olympics in 2008 will be held in which of the following cities?

(A) Athens

(B) Baghdad

(C) Torino

(D) Beijing

487. What are the only two cities to have hosted two different Winter Olympics?

(A) St. Moritz and Innsbruck

(B) Innsbruck and Calgary

(C) St. Moritz and Lake Placid

(D) Innsbruck and Lake Placid

488. Which of the following were the first televised Olympic games?

(A) Berlin, 1936

(B) Helsinki, 1952

(C) Melbourne, 1956

(D) Munich, 1972

489. What was unusual about the fact that Holland's Fanny Blankers-Koen won four track and field gold medals in 1948?

(A) She was 48 years old.

(B) She was the 30-year old mother of two.

(C) She had never competed in her medal-winning events before the Olympics.

(D) She was the only competitor in each event.

490. Which of the following is the largest city to ever host the Olympic games?

(A) Los Angeles

(B) Paris

(C) London

(D) Mexico City

491. What was unusual about the 1900 Paris games?

(A) There were not enough medals to give to all the medal winners.

(B) There were more athletes than spectators.

(C) There were riots by spectators trying to fill standing-room-only areas.

(D) There were riots by the soccer spectators.

492. In which Olympics did a bomb explode, killing one and injuring many others?

(A) Moscow, 1980

(B) Los Angeles, 1984

(C) Atlanta, 1996

(D) Sydney, 2000

493. Why was Jim Thorpe originally stripped of his Olympic medals?

(A) He went to jail for running moonshine.

(B) He went to jail for robbing a bank.

(C) It was discovered that he was Native American.

(D) It was discovered that he played semi-pro baseball for a short time.

494. In which year did China first participate in the Olympics?

(A) 1896

(B) 1900

(C) 1984

(D) 1988

495. What movie tells the tale of two British runners, one a Christian from Scotland and the other a Jew from England, who compete in the 1924 Olympics?

(A) *Kramer vs. Kramer*

(B) *The Longest Yard*

(C) *Logan's Run*

(D) *Chariots of Fire*

496. The phrase *"citius, altius, fortius,"* which is often associated with the Olympics, translates as which of the following?

(A) Swifter, higher, stronger

(B) Bigger, stronger, faster

(C) Cities, countries, continents

(D) Cities, athletes, countries

497. Which of the following actually is a figure skating move named for a U.S. Olympic skater?

(A) The Hamilton Hike

(B) The Kwan Quad

(C) The Hamill Camel

(D) The Boitano Blast

498. Who is the most decorated U.S. Winter Olympian?

(A) Eric Heiden

(B) Bonnie Blair

(C) Dan Jansen

(D) Michelle Kwan

499. Former USFL and NFL star Herschel Walker competed in which Olympic event?

(A) Decathlon

(B) Hammer throw

(C) Discus throw

(D) Bobsled

500. In what year was the first electric timing device used in the Olympics?

(A) 1896

(B) 1912

(C) 1936

(D) 1952

501. When were Iranian women first allowed, by their government, to participate in the Olympics?

(A) 1936

(B) 1976

(C) 1980

(D) 1996

502. What are the only two countries from the southern hemisphere that have won medals in the Winter Olympics?

(A) Brazil and Argentina

(B) Argentina and South Africa

(C) South Africa and Australia

(D) Australia and New Zealand

503. During which Olympics did Arab commandos kill two and take nine other Israeli athletes hostage only to kill them later in a shootout?

(A) Munich, 1972

(B) Montreal, 1976

(C) Moscow, 1980

(D) Los Angeles, 1984

504. Which country always leads the athletes into the opening ceremonies at the Olympics?

(A) The host country

(B) The country that hosted the last Olympics

(C) The country who won the most medals in the last Olympics

(D) Greece

505. Which country always enters the opening ceremonies last at the Olympics?

(A) The host country

(B) The country that hosted the last Olympics

(C) The country that won the most medals in the last Olympics

(D) The country that won the fewest medals in the last Olympics

506. Phillip Noel-Baker won the silver medal in the 1500m at the 1920 Olympic games in Antwerp then went on to win which of the following in 1959?

(A) The gold medal in the 1500m

(B) The gold medal in the 100m

(C) The gold medal in the biathlon

(D) The Nobel Peace Prize

507. What interesting fact do Australia, Great Britain, Greece, France, and Switzerland all have in common?

(A) These are the only nations that have won more than 100 total Olympic medals.

(B) These are the only nations that have hosted both Summer and Winter Olympics.

(C) These are the only nations that have participated in every Summer Olympics since 1896.

(D) These are the only nations that have been banned from and then reinstated to the Olympics.

508. The Nordic Combined is a combination of which two events?

 (A) Platform diving and springboard diving

 (B) Archery and horseback riding

 (C) Cross-county skiing and target shooting

 (D) Ski jumping and cross-country skiing

509. Who is most often credited with beginning the modern Olympic games?

 (A) Woodrow Wilson

 (B) Theodore Roosevelt

 (C) Pierre de Cubertin

 (D) Catherine the Great

510. What sort of Olympic event is the skeleton?

 (A) An Australian game using a modified boomerang

 (B) An event similar to luge but where riders go down the track head first

 (C) A rowing event with three rowers and one rider

 (D) An equestrian event

511. What is unusual about all the medals awarded at the 2002 Winter Olympics in Salt Lake City?

 (A) All the medals were solid gold, silver, or bronze.

 (B) All the medals were plated with gold, silver, or bronze.

 (C) All the metal for the medals was mined in Utah.

 (D) All the metal for the medals was left over from the Atlanta games in 1996.

512. What is the Olympic motto?

 (A) "The important thing is not the triumph, but the struggle."

 (B) "Swifter, higher, stronger"

 (C) It is not to win, but to take part."

 (D) "The essential thing is not to have conquered, but to have fought well."

513. During the closing parade of the Olympics, in what order do the athletes enter the stadium?

(A) Unlike the opening parade, the athletes are not separated in national teams.

(B) They are separated by country, in the order of the medals won.

(C) The host team enters first, with the rest of the teams in alphabetical order.

(D) The host team enters last, with the rest of the teams in alphabetical order.

CHAPTER 10 ANSWERS

462. **The correct answer is (B).** The first Olympic games were held in the shadow of Mount Olympus in ancient Greece.

463. **The correct answer is (C).** The first Olympic games since the fourth century C.E. were held in Athens in 1896 and consisted of only summer events.

464. **The correct answer is (D).** The first Winter Olympics were not held until 1924.

465. **The correct answer is (A).** The five rings are blue, green, yellow, red, and black and they symbolize nations of all five inhabited continents.

466. **The correct answer is (B).** The Olympic torch was first carried into the opening ceremonies at the 1928 Olympic games and has been a tradition ever since.

467. **The correct answer is (D).** The tug-of-war was an official Olympic event from 1900 to 1920.

468. **The correct answer is (D).** The United States sent no Olympic athletes to the 1980 games in Moscow to protest the 1979 Soviet invasion of Afghanistan.

469. **The correct answer is (B).** Because of World War II (1939–1945), the Summer and Winter games of 1944 were cancelled.

470. **The correct answer is (C).** The only three to ever accomplish this feat were America's Eddie Eagan, Norway's Jacob Tullin Tham, and East Germany's Christa Luding-Rothenberger.

471. **The correct answer is (D).** Mark Spitz won four golds for individual events and three golds for relays and he set a new world record time in each event.

472. **The correct answer is (C).** The United States has won more track and field medals than the next two countries combined.

473. **The correct answer is (A).** The pentathlon consists of running a 4000 meter course, riding horseback through an obstacle course, swimming a freestyle heat, fencing against another competitor, and shooting air pistols at targets.

474. **The correct answer is (B).** Jim Thorpe won both events in 1912 and said, "Thanks, King," when the king of Sweden said that he was the greatest athlete in the world.

475. **The correct answer is (D).** Dick Fosbury, an Olympic high jumper, invented the technique as a better way to clear the high jump bar.

476. **The correct answer is (A).** Totally wrapped up in dreams of an Aryan nation, Hitler refused to the shake the hand of Jesse Owens, an African-American athlete, when he won a gold medal in Berlin.

477. **The correct answer is (C).** In 1936, Germany secretly and illegally entered a man with the alias of Dora Ratjen in the women's high jump but still did not take home a medal for the event.

478. **The correct answer is (A).** The Scandinavian countries did not want a separate Olympic games in the Winter for fear that the Winter Olympics would threaten the Nordic Games, a Scandinavian tradition.

479. **The correct answer is (B).** The "Miracle on Ice" occurred when the U.S. hockey team knocked off the Soviet team on their way to winning the gold medal in the 1980 Winter Olympics in Lake Placid, New York.

480. **The correct answer is (D).** The Jamaican bobsled team was featured in the comedic movie *Cool Runnings*.

481. **The correct answer is (D).** Snowboarding made its Olympic debut at the 1988 Winter Olympics in Nagano, Japan.

482. **The correct answer is (A).** The axel is the only forward-facing jump and arguably is the easiest to do and to recognize.

483. The correct answer is (B). Tara Lipinski was only 15 years old when she won the gold in 1998.

484. The correct answer is (D). Eddie "the Eagle" was Great Britain's only ski jumper in the 1988 Olympics and he finished 56th out 57 entries. However, Eddie was easily the fan favorite for his sheer determination.

485. The correct answer is (C). Golf has only been an official Olympic sport twice, in 1900 and in 1904.

486. The correct answer is (D). The XXIX Olympiad will be held in Beijing, China, in 2008.

487. The correct answer is (A). St. Moritz hosted in 1928 and 1948, and Innsbruck hosted in 1964 and 1976.

488. The correct answer is (A). The 1936 Summer Olympics in Berlin were the first ever televised.

489. The correct answer is (B). It was a 30-year old mother of two children who won four gold medals while competing against women much younger than she.

490. The correct answer is (D). Mexico City, the largest city in the world, hosted the 1968 Summer Olympics.

491. The correct answer is (B). There were actually more athletes participating in the 1900 Olympics than there were spectators watching them.

492. The correct answer is (C). A bomb exploded in the Olympic Plaza in Atlanta in 1996; the bomber, Eric Rudolph, was apprehended in 2003.

493. The correct answer is (D). Thorpe spent a short stint in semi-professional baseball and he was forced to forfeit his medals when that was discovered.

494. The correct answer is (C). China first participated in the Olympics in 1984 in Los Angeles.

495. The correct answer is (D). *Chariots of Fire* actually won Best Picture in 1981.

496. The correct answer is (A). The Latin phrase translates as "swifter, higher, stronger" and is often used as a credo for Olympic athletes.

497. The correct answer is (C). The Hamill Camel is named for skater Dorothy Hamill.

498. The correct answer is (B). Speed skater Bonnie Blair has won five gold medals and one bronze medal in her Olympic career.

499. The correct answer is (D). Herschel Walker was a member of the 1992 U.S. bobsled team.

500. The correct answer is (B). An electronic timing device, along with a public address system, was first employed at the 1912 Olympic Games in Stockholm.

501. The correct answer is (D). Iranian women first competed for Iran in the 1996 Olympics in Atlanta.

502. The correct answer is (D). Australia and New Zealand are the only medal-winning nations from the southern hemisphere.

503. The correct answer is (A). The tragedy stopped the games for 24 hours but the IOC determined "the games must go on."

504. The correct answer is (D). Greece always leads the athletes into the opening ceremonies.

505. The correct answer is (A). The host country always brings up the rear of the athletes' processional into the opening ceremonies.

506. The correct answer is (D). Phillip Noel-Baker won the Nobel Peace Prize in 1959.

507. The correct answer is (C). Each of these five nations has participated in every Summer Olympics since 1896.

508. The correct answer is (D). Nordic combined is a combination of ski jumping and cross-country skiing and has been an Olympic event since 1924.

509. The correct answer is (C). Pierre de Coubertin believed the Olympic games might help the world's nations toward more peaceful relations.

510. The correct answer is (B). The skeleton is very much like luge, but the skeleton riders ride head first down an icy track.

511. The correct answer is (C). All the medals awarded at the 2002 Salt Lake City Olympic Games were made from metal that was mined in Utah.

512. The correct answer is (B). The others are part of the Olympic creed.

513. The correct answer is (A). To symbolize the unity and friendship of the games, the athletics are not separated into national teams as they enter the stadium to symbolize the unity and friendship of the games. This tradition began at the 1956 Melbourne Olympics.

CHAPTER 11

On the Sidelines: Coaches

514. What legendary football coach is the subject of the book and the movie titled *The Junction Boys*?

(A) Paul "Bear" Bryant

(B) George Halas

(C) Paul Brown

(D) Eddie Robinson

515. What NBA head coach is famous for his fascination with Zen philosophy?

(A) Pat Riley

(B) Red Auerbach

(C) Chuck Daley

(D) Phil Jackson

I'm not as smart as other coaches; I have to work harder.
—PAUL "BEAR" BRYANT

516. Who is the all-time winningest coach in NHL history with more than 1,100 wins?

(A)   Toe Blake

(B)   Scotty Bowman

(C)   Glen Sather

(D)   Pat Burns

517. The NFL's Super Bowl trophy is named after which legendary coach?

(A)   Paul Brown

(B)   George Halas

(C)   Bum Phillips

(D)   Vince Lombardi

518. What fiery coach managed the Baltimore Orioles and is remembered most for his temper?

(A)   Eddie Murray

(B)   Sparky Anderson

(C)   Earl Weaver

(D)   Tommy Lasorda

519. Which of the following NCAA basketball coaches is referred to as "the General"?

(A)   Rick Pitino

(B)   Bob Huggins

(C)   Adolph Rupp

(D)   Bobby Knight

520. Who was the cigar-smoking coach of the Boston Celtics during the Celtics' dynasty?

(A)   John Wooden

(B)   Red Auerbach

(C)   Phil Jackson

(D)   Pat Riley

521. Which Yankees' skipper is remembered for his on-again, off-again relationship with Yankees' owner George Steinbrenner?

(A) Joe Torre

(B) Joe McCarthy

(C) Billy Martin

(D) Lou Piniella

522. Who was the first coach of the Dallas Cowboys?

(A) Paul Bryant

(B) Jimmy Johnson

(C) Barry Switzer

(D) Tom Landry

523. NCAA basketball coach Jerry Tarkanian is famous for biting which of the following during his games?

(A) A towel

(B) His fingers

(C) His assistant coach

(D) His clipboard

524. Which of the following former NBA stars came out of retirement to coach his former NBA team in the 1993–94 season?

(A) Michael Jordan

(B) Larry Bird

(C) Kevin McHale

(D) Magic Johnson

525. Who is the only NCAA women's basketball coach to coach one team to two undefeated seasons?

(A) Geno Auriemma

(B) Pat Summitt

(C) Jody Conradt

(D) Muffet McGraw

526. The MLB manager who holds the career record for regular seasons wins is which of the following?

(A) Sparky Anderson

(B) Casey Stengel

(C) Connie Mack

(D) Joe McCarthy

527. Knute Rockne was a legendary football coach at which of the following universities?

(A) Harvard

(B) Yale

(C) Ohio State

(D) Notre Dame

528. What NFL coach may be remembered most for his tendency to weep openly during press conferences and other occasions?

(A) Jim Mora

(B) Chuck Noll

(C) Dick Vermeil

(D) John Madden

529. Who is the all-time winningest men's NCAA Division I basketball coach?

(A) Adolph Rupp

(B) Claire Bee

(C) Jim Calhoun

(D) Dean Smith

530. Which gymnastics coach trained such athletes as Nadia Comaneci, Mary Lou Retton, and Dominique Moceanu?

(A) Romeo Neri

(B) Boris Shakhlin

(C) Bela Karolyi

(D) Dmitri Bilozerchev

531. Which coach won a national championship in football at the University of Miami before moving on to the Dallas Cowboys where he also won the Super Bowl?

(A) Tom Landry

(B) Dave Campo

(C) Jimmy Johnson

(D) Butch Davis

532. Who holds the major league record for World Series appearances, World Series games won, and World Series championships?

(A) Connie Mack

(B) Walter Alston

(C) Tommy Lasorda

(D) Casey Stengel

533. Who is the NBA's all-time winningest coach?

(A) Lenny Wilkens

(B) Don Nelson

(C) Red Auerbach

(D) Phil Jackson

534. Which baseball manager is famous for such lines as, "It ain't over 'til it's over," and "It's like deja vu all over again"?

(A) Tommy Lasorda

(B) Earl Weaver

(C) Buck Showalter

(D) Yogi Berra

535. What NFL coach is nicknamed "the Tuna"?

(A) Steve Walsh

(B) Steve Mariucci

(C) Mike Holmgren

(D) Bill Parcells

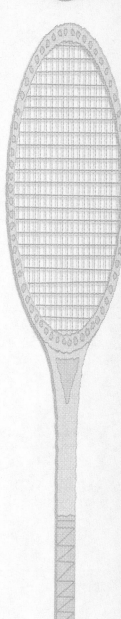

536. Who is the only manager to win the World Series in both leagues?

(A) Sparky Anderson

(B) Tony LaRussa

(C) Billy Martin

(D) Billy Williams

537. Who played Coach Norman Dale of Hickory, Indiana, in the classic basketball movie *Hoosiers*?

(A) Tommy Lee Jones

(B) Gene Hackman

(C) John Lithgow

(D) Nick Nolte

538. Who is the NCAA all-time winningest football coach (any division)?

(A) Joe Paterno

(B) Paul "Bear" Bryant

(C) Bobby Bowden

(D) Eddie Robinson

539. Which of the following coaches won a Stanley Cup with Chicago, Detroit, and Toronto as a player, then coached the New York Islanders to four consecutive Cups?

(A) Scotty Bowman

(B) Mike Keenan

(C) Al Arbour

(D) Glen Sather

540. What tennis coach runs an academy that has produced such stars as Andre Agassi, Monica Seles, and Jim Courier?

(A) Richard Williams

(B) Nick Bolletieri

(C) Vic Braden

(D) Don Budge

541. What former NFL coach who holds the NFL record for seasons coached was nicknamed "Papa Bear"?

(A) Vince Lombardi

(B) Paul Brown

(C) George Halas

(D) Tom Landry

542. Which of the following awards recognizes leadership qualities and contribution to the community and is named for a former NHL coach?

(A) The Stanley Cup

(B) The Calder Memorial Trophy

(C) The James Norris Memorial Trophy

(D) The Clancy Trophy

543. Where did the legendary Phog Allen coach men's college basketball?

(A) Kansas

(B) Iowa State

(C) Kentucky

(D) Texas

544. How many national championships did John Wooden's basketball teams win for UCLA?

(A) 0

(B) 5

(C) 10

(D) 20

545. Who coached the Buffalo Bills to four Super Bowls only to lose all four games?

(A) Mike Shanahan

(B) Marv Levy

(C) Bill Parcells

(D) June Jones

546. What other NFL team besides the Chicago Bears did Mike Ditka coach?

(A) Minnesota Vikings

(B) Detroit Lions

(C) Tampa Bay Buccaneers

(D) New Orleans Saints

547. Who is the only coach to win titles in both the NFL and the AFL?

(A) Weeb Ewbank

(B) Paul Brown

(C) Vince Lombardi

(D) Tom Landry

548. Legendary college basketball coach Clarence Gaines was commonly known by which of the following nicknames?

(A) "Big Daddy"

(B) "Big Pappa"

(C) "Big Clarence"

(D) "Big House"

549. Who was forced to resign from his post at Ohio State after striking an opposing player in the 1978 Gator Bowl?

(A) Bobby Bowden

(B) Bill Curry

(C) Woody Hayes

(D) Bo Schembechler

550. Who is the all-time winningest active MLB manager in regular season wins?

(A) Lou Piniella

(B) Joe Torre

(C) Tony LaRussa

(D) Bobby Cox

551. What legendary basketball coach coached Oklahoma
A&M (later, Oklahoma State) from 1934 to 1970, won
two national titles, and ranks fourth all-time in wins?

(A) Roy Williams

(B) Hank Iba

(C) Eddie Sutton

(D) Phog Allen

552. Curly Lambeau coached what NFL team to three titles
during his 29-year tenure?

(A) The Green Bay Packers

(B) The Dallas Cowboys

(C) The Chicago Bears

(D) The Detroit Lions

553. NCAA basketball coach John Thompson, known for
producing such great centers as Ewing, Mutumbo,
and Mourning, coached at which of the following
universities where he won the national title in 1984?

(A) Loyola-Marymount

(B) UNLV

(C) UCLA

(D) Georgetown

554. Which of the following awards is the NHL equivalent to
Coach of the Year?

(A) The Selke Trophy

(B) The Lady Byng Memorial Trophy

(C) The Adams Award

(D) The Conn Smythe Trophy

555. Who is generally credited for devising the short passing
game known the West Coast Offense?

(A) Mike Holmgren

(B) Norv Turner

(C) Steve Mariucci

(D) Bill Walsh

556. Which of the following is *not* true of coaching legend Amos Alonzo Stagg?

(A) His career spanned from 1892 to 1946.

(B) He never won a national championship.

(C) He is the only coach in both the college football and college basketball Halls of Fame.

(D) He was named Coach of the Year in 1943 at the age of 81.

557. Who coached the only undefeated NFL team in history?

(A) Paul Brown

(B) Curly Lambeau

(C) Vince Lombardi

(D) Don Shula

558. Which hockey coach improved the design of the modern net and puck and has the NHL scoring champion's trophy named after him?

(A) Art Ross

(B) Scotty Bowman

(C) Lord Stanley

(D) Conn Smythe

559. What MLB manager led the U.S. Olympic baseball team to an unlikely gold medal in the 2000 Olympic Games in Sydney?

(A) Joe Torre

(B) Art Howe

(C) Tommy Lasorda

(D) Felipe Alou

560. Which of the following was the real name of the famous baseball coach Connie Mack?

(A) Connie Mack

(B) Cornelius Mack

(C) Cornelius McGillicuddy

(D) Conn MacGinnis

561. Which NFL coach led his team to four Super Bowls in six years?

(A) Jimmy Johnson

(B) Tom Landry

(C) Bill Walsh

(D) Chuck Noll

562. Who was the first manager to win a pennant in both leagues in MLB?

(A) Joe McCarthy

(B) Casey Stengel

(C) Billy Martin

(D) Tony LaRussa

563. Which of the following college basketball coaching greats is known as "Doctor"?

(A) Al McGuire

(B) Dean Smith

(C) Jack Ramsay

(D) John Wooden

564. With which NBA franchise did Bill Fitch record his 1,000th victory as a head coach?

(A) Dallas Mavericks

(B) Atlanta Hawks

(C) Boston Celtics

(D) Los Angeles Clippers

CHAPTER 11 ANSWERS

514. The correct answer is (A). *The Junction Boys* is about Texas A&M football coach Paul "Bear" Bryant during the football camp at Junction, Texas.

515. The correct answer is (D). Phil Jackson, who won championships in Chicago and Los Angeles, is known for his Zen philosophy and his fascination with Buddhist thought.

516. The correct answer is (B). Scotty Bowman is the only NHL coach with more than 1,000 wins, and he earned them with five different teams.

517. The correct answer is (D). The Lombardi Trophy is awarded annually to the NFL's Super Bowl winner.

518. The correct answer is (C). Earl Weaver coached the Orioles from 1968 to 1982 and then again from 1985 to 1986.

519. The correct answer is (D). Bobby Knight became known as "the General" at Indiana, but he now coaches at Texas Tech.

520. The correct answer is (B). Red Auerbach coached the Celtics during their dynasty years in the 1960s.

521. The correct answer is (C). Billy Martin was hired and fired repeatedly by George Steinbrenner during his time with the Yankees.

522. The correct answer is (D). Tom Landry coached the Dallas Cowboys for more than thirty years and was the original Cowboys coach.

523. The correct answer is (A). Tarkanian became known for chewing a towel during his coaching days at UNLV.

524. The correct answer is (D). Magic Johnson coached the Lakers, his former team, for sixteen games during the 1993–94 season.

525. The correct answer is (A). Geno Auriemma coached the UConn Lady Huskies to perfect seasons in 1994–95 and in 2001–02.

526. The correct answer is (C). Connie Mack notched 3,755 wins in 53 years.

527. The correct answer is (D). Knute Rockne coached the Irish from 1918 to 1930.

528. The correct answer is (C). Reporters look forward to press conferences with Dick Vermeil because he will probably cry about something.

529. The correct answer is (D). Dean Smith has 879 career victories, all at the University of North Carolina.

530. The correct answer is (C). A native of Romania, Bella Karolyi moved to the United States where he became the driving force behind women's gymnastics in America.

531. The correct answer is (C). Jimmy Johnson won the national title in Miami in 1987 and then won the Super Bowl with the Cowboys in 1993 and in 1994.

532. The correct answer is (D). Casey Stengel won 37 World Series games and 7 World Series championships in 10 World Series appearances.

533. The correct answer is (A). Lenny Wilkins has more than 1,250 wins heading into the 2002–03 season.

534. The correct answer is (D). Long-time catcher and manager for the Yankees, Yogi Berra is notorious for his double-speak and nonsensical quotes.

535. The correct answer is (D). Bill Parcells is affectionately known by his fans as "the Tuna."

536. The correct answer is (A). Sparky Anderson won the World Series with the Reds in 1975 and 1976 and with the Tigers in 1984.

537. The correct answer is (B). Gene Hackman played Norman Dale in the true story of Hickory's unlikely run to the Indiana state basketball championship.

538. The correct answer is (D). Eddie Robinson retired with the all-time college record of 408 career wins at Grambling State University in Louisiana.

539. The correct answer is (C). Al Arbour coached the NY Islanders to the Stanley Cup championship from 1980 to 1983.

540. The correct answer is (B). Nick Bolletieri has run Nick Bolletieri Tennis Academy since 1976 in Brandenton, Florida.

541. The correct answer is (C). George Halas, also known as "Papa Bear," coached an amazing forty seasons in the NFL.

542. The correct answer is (D). The Clancy Trophy is named in honor of King Clancy, former coach of the Montreal Maroons.

543. The correct answer is (A). Phog Allen spent most of his career at Kansas and retired in 1956.

544. The correct answer is (C). John Wooden won ten championships in twelve years while coaching at UCLA and is the only person in the Basketball Hall of Fame as a coach and a player.

545. The correct answer is (B). Marv Levy led the Bills to four Super Bowls from 1991 to 1994 but lost every one of them.

546. The correct answer is (D). Mike Ditka coached the Chicago Bears to a Super Bowl championship in 1985, but had far less success during his tenure with the Saints.

547. The correct answer is (A). Weeb Ewbank coached the Baltimore Colts to an AFL title in 1958 and coached the New York Jets to victory in Super Bowl III.

548. The correct answer is (D). Clarence "Big House" Gaines won more than 800 games at Winston-Salem during his career.

549. The correct answer is (C). Woody Hayes was forced to resign despite winning three national titles and four Rose Bowls.

550. The correct answer is (C). Tony LaRussa leads all active managers in regular season wins, followed by Bobby Cox, and then by Joe Torre.

551. The correct answer is (B). Hank Iba won national titles in 1945 and 1946; OSU's basketball arena is named for Iba.

552. The correct answer is (A). Curly Lambeau is the great Packers coach for whom the Packers' Lambeau Field is named.

553. The correct answer is (D). John Thompson also produced a great guard in Allen Iverson and was runner-up for the national title in 1982 and 1985.

554. The correct answer is (C). The Adams Award is awarded annually "to the NHL coach adjudged to have contributed the most to his team's success." The trophy is named in honor of Jack Adams, longtime coach and general manager of the Red Wings.

555. The correct answer is (D). Bill Walsh developed the West Coast Offense and made it an integral part of the San Francisco 49ers' offensive scheme in the 1980s.

556. The correct answer is (B). Stagg won a national title in 1905 with Chicago.

557. The correct answer is (D). Don Shula coached the 1972 Miami Dolphins, the only NFL team to go an entire season undefeated.

558. The correct answer is (A). Art Ross won the Stanley Cup in 1938 and in 1939 and is the namesake of the NHL's award for the annual scoring champion.

559. The correct answer is (C). Tommy Lasorda, former coach of the Los Angeles Dodgers led the U.S. Olympic team to an Olympic championship in 2000.

560. The correct answer is (C). Connie Mack was actually born Cornelius McGillicuddy in 1862.

561. The correct answer is (D). Chuck Noll took the Pittsburgh Steelers to the Super Bowl in 1975, 1976, 1979, and 1980.

562. The correct answer is (A). Joe McCarthy won with Chicago of the NL in 1929 and with New York of the AL in 1932.

563. The correct answer is (C). "Doctor" Jack Ramsay coached the basketball team at St. Joseph's, and he coached the NBA's Portland Trailblazers to the 1977 NBA title; he currently broadcasts NBA basketball games.

564. The correct answer is (D). Bill Fitch recorded his 1,000[th] victory as a head coach while he was coach of the Los Angeles Clippers. He coached the Clippers from 1995 to 1998. In 1997, Fitch was named one of the Ten Greatest Coaches.

CHAPTER 12

A Plaque on the Wall:
Hall of Famers

565. What color are the blazers worn by Pro Football Hall of Fame inductees?

(A) Green

(B) Yellow

(C) Black

(D) Blue

566. Which of the following Baseball Hall of Famers is the only member to hit a pinch-hit grand slam in a World Series game?

(A) Yogi Berra

(B) Willie Mays

(C) Rod Carew

(D) Harmon Killebrew

Today, I'm joining the greatest team of all.
—JIM KELLY

567. Which of the following basketball icons are members of the Basketball Hall of Fame as both a player and a coach?

(A)   John Wooden and Bobby Knight

(B)   Lenny Wilkens and Phil Jackson

(C)   John Wooden and Lenny Wilkens

(D)   Phil Jackson and Bobby Knight

568. Which Hall of Fame coach led his team to victory in the "Ice Bowl," a game widely regarded as the greatest football game of all time?

(A)   Paul Brown

(B)   Vince Lombardi

(C)   Tom Landry

(D)   Chuck Noll

569. Which Hall of Famer scored the winning touchdown in the "Ice Bowl"?

(A)   Dan Reeves

(B)   Ray Nitschke

(C)   Bart Starr

(D)   None of the above

570. About which Hockey Hall of Famer was said, "(his) record book is now complete. He's the all-time leader in points, assists, and now with his 802nd goal, the all-time leading goal scorer"?

(A)   Bobby Hull

(B)   Gordie Howe

(C)   Bobby Orr

(D)   Wayne Gretzky

571. Which Hall of Famer hit a Game 7 bottom-of-the-ninth World Series-winning homer in 1960 to topple the mighty New York Yankees?

(A) Bobby Thompson

(B) Stan Musial

(C) Johnny Mize

(D) Bill Mazeroski

572. Which Auto Racing Hall of Famer won his 200th race on July 4, 1984?

(A) Cale Yarborough

(B) Richard Petty

(C) Dale Earnhardt

(D) Ned Jarrett

573. Which Hall of Famer did Magic Johnson play against in the 1979 NCAA championship game?

(A) Moses Malone

(B) Isiah Thomas

(C) Larry Bird

(D) Julius Erving

574. Which Pro Baseball Hall of Famer is perhaps best remembered for trying to wave a 1975 World Series homerun fair along the left field line?

(A) Carlton Fisk

(B) Willie McCovey

(C) Johnny Bench

(D) Tony Perez

575. Which Hall of Fame tennis great is the only Aboriginal Australian in the International Tennis Hall of Fame?

(A) Rod Laver

(B) Evonne Goolagong

(C) Martina Navratilova

(D) Mats Wilander

576. Which Hall of Famer guaranteed a victory in Super Bowl III despite his team being the underdog?

(A) Johnny Unitas

(B) Bart Starr

(C) Joe Namath

(D) Len Dawson

577. Which Basketball Hall of Famer is often regarded as the best sixth man in the history of the NBA?

(A) Calvin Murphy

(B) Elvin Hayes

(C) Bob Cousy

(D) John Havlicek

578. Which Hall of Fame soccer player came out of retirement in 1975 to sign with the New York Cosmos, thus creating a huge surge in youth soccer participation in the United States?

(A) Pele

(B) Pat McBride

(C) Archie Stark

(D) Jimmy Roe

579. Which NFL franchise boasts the most Hall of Famers?

(A) Chicago Bears

(B) Green Bay Packers

(C) New York Giants

(D) Dallas Cowboys

580. Which of the following Hall of Fame starting pitchers was a reliever during the 1969 World Series for the Miracle Mets?

(A) Tom Seaver

(B) Steve Carlton

(C) Don Drysdale

(D) Nolan Ryan

581. Which of the following members of the 1980 U.S. Olympic hockey team that played in the "Miracle on Ice" is now in the Hockey Hall of Fame?

(A) Jim Craig

(B) Dave Christian

(C) Mike Eruzione

(D) None of the U.S. players have made it to the Hockey Hall of Fame.

582. Which Hall of Famer is the only other player besides Wilt Chamberlain to be named Rookie of the Year and MVP in the same season?

(A) Nate Thurmond

(B) Nate Archibald

(C) Bill Russell

(D) Wes Unseld

583. Which of the following Hall of Fame tennis legends was the first woman to win 1,000 singles matches and 150 tournaments?

(A) Billie Jean King

(B) Alice Marble

(C) Chris Evert

(D) Helen Wills Moody

584. Hall of Fame player Ty Cobb coached which of the following teams following his playing career?

(A) Detroit Tigers

(B) New York Yankees

(C) Cleveland Indians

(D) Chicago Cubs

585. Which Pro Football Hall of Famer made the "Immaculate Reception"?

(A) John Stallworth

(B) Lynn Swann

(C) Franco Harris

(D) Steve Largent

586. Which Hall of Famer threw the touchdown pass that came to be known as "The Catch"?

(A) Joe Montana

(B) Roger Staubach

(C) Terry Bradshaw

(D) Johnny Unitas

587. Which Hockey Hall of Famer holds the record for games played?

(A) Tim Horton

(B) Gordie Howe

(C) Wayne Gretzky

(D) John Bucyk

588. Hall of Famer Willie Mays got his first major league hit, a homer, off which Hall of Fame pitcher?

(A) Robin Roberts

(B) Bob Feller

(C) Warren Spahn

(D) Sandy Koufax

589. Which of the following teams is enshrined in the Basketball Hall of Fame?

(A) Boston Celtics

(B) Minneapolis Lakers

(C) Springfield (Massachusetts) YMCA

(D) Harlem Globetrotters

590. Which of the following Hockey Hall of Famers did *not* play goalie?

(A) Terry Sawchuk

(B) Jacques Plante

(C) Bernie Parent

(D) Denis Savard

591. Which of the following former U.S. Presidents shares a name with a member of the International Boxing Hall of Fame?

(A) Jimmy Carter

(B) George Bush

(C) John Adams

(D) John Kennedy

592. As of 2002, which of the following is the only placekicker in the Pro Football Hall of Fame?

(A) Tom Dempsey

(B) Jan Stenerud

(C) Gary Andersen

(D) Matt Stover

593. Which World Golf Hall of Fame member is best remembered for his golf instruction books, *The Little Red Book* and *The Little Green Book*?

(A) Byron Nelson

(B) Sam Snead

(C) Harvey Penick

(D) Ben Hogan

594. Which of the following Baseball Hall of Famers was the oldest player to win the MVP award?

(A) Willie Stargell

(B) Babe Ruth

(C) Hank Aaron

(D) Willie Mays

595. Which Hall of Famer was a Davis Cup singles and doubles legend and had his own line of tennis shoes in the 1980s?

(A) Bjorn Borg

(B) Stan Smith

(C) Ken McGregor

(D) Rod Laver

596. What is significant about Morgan Wootten's enshrinement in the Basketball Hall of Fame?

(A) Wootten never played basketball.

(B) Wootten never saw a basketball game because he is blind.

(C) Wootten never heard a basketball game because he is deaf.

(D) Wootten coached high school basketball his entire career.

597. Which Hockey Hall of Famer holds the record for the most trophies won in a season?

(A) Wayne Gretzky

(B) Bobby Orr

(C) Stan Mikita

(D) Guy Lafleur

598. Which of the following Hall of Famers finished his career with a home run in his last at bat?

(A) Ted Williams

(B) Hank Aaron

(C) George Brett

(D) Reggie Jackson

599. Which Hall of Fame runningback was the first player to ever reach the 2,000 yard single-season rushing mark?

(A) Jim Brown

(B) O. J. Simpson

(C) Gale Sayers

(D) Red Grange

600. Which Hall of Fame hoopster broke Wilt Chamberlain's NBA career scoring record in 1984 and still holds the NBA's career scoring mark?

(A) Kareem Abdul-Jabbar

(B) Elvin Hayes

(C) Oscar Robertson

(D) John Havlicek

601. Baseball's Rookie of the Year Award is named for which of the following players, the first to win the award in 1947?

(A) Warren Spahn

(B) Joe DiMaggio

(C) Roger Maris

(D) Jackie Robinson

602. Which Hockey Hall of Famer holds the record for most career Art Ross Trophies and for most career Hart Memorial Trophies?

(A) Bobby Orr

(B) Wayne Gretzky

(C) Bobby Hull

(D) Gordie Howe

603. Which Hall of Fame boxer knocked out the German Max Schmeling in the first round of their rematch in what was called one of the worst beatings in boxing history?

(A) Jersey Joe Walcott

(B) Jack Dempsey

(C) Joe Louis

(D) Archie Moore

604. Which International Tennis Hall of Famer suffered an embarrassing defeat in the infamous "Battle of the Sexes" tennis match in 1973?

(A) Don Budge

(B) Bobby Riggs

(C) Rod Laver

(D) Bill Tilden

605. Which Hall of Fame footballer was the oldest player ever to appear in a professional football game?

(A) Johnny Unitas

(B) George Blanda

(C) Norm Snead

(D) Dan Fouts

606. Which member of the College Football Hall of Fame was the subject of a great motivational speech once given by Knute Rockne?

(A) Ziggy Czarobski

(B) Dan Devine

(C) George Gipp

(D) Elmer Layden

607. Which of the following Hall of Famers was the youngest baseball player ever to be named MVP?

(A) Johnny Bench

(B) Reggie Jackson

(C) Ted Williams

(D) Willie McCovey

608. Which Basketball Hall of Famer once made forty consecutive free throws and had his number 25 retired by the Lakers in 1996?

(A) James Worthy

(B) Magic Johnson

(C) Gail Goodrich

(D) Wilt Chamberlain

609. Which member of the World Golf Hall of Fame not only won thirty-one tournaments in her career but also won two Olympic track and field medals in 1932?

(A) Babe Didrikson Zaharias

(B) Patty Berg

(C) Mickey Wright

(D) Louise Suggs

610. Which member of the Figure Skating Hall of Fame is one of only two figure skaters to receive the AAU Sullivan Award for outstanding U.S. Amateur Athlete?

(A) Dorothy Hamill

(B) Sonja Henie

(C) Dick Buttons

(D) Peggy Fleming

611. Which Hall of Famer is often regarded as the best lefthander ever to play tennis?

(A) Jimmy Connors

(B) John McEnroe

(C) Ivan Lendl

(D) Arthur Ashe

612. Which of the following Hockey Hall of Famers was elected to the most career All-Star games?

(A) Wayne Gretzky

(B) Maurice Richard

(C) Gordie Howe

(D) Bobby Hull

613. Which of the following is *not* actually a nickname of a Pro Football Hall of Famer?

(A) Crazylegs

(B) Tuffy

(C) Shorty

(D) Crusher

614. Which of the following Hall of Fame pitchers never won the Cy Young Award?

(A) Steve Carlton

(B) Bob Gibson

(C) warren Spahn

(D) Juan Marichal

615. Which Hall of Famer was also an All-American basketball player in college?

(A) Lou Boudreau

(B) Lou Gehrig

(C) Hank Aaron

(D) Dave Winfield

CHAPTER 12 ANSWERS

565. The correct answer is (B). Pro Football Hall of Fame inductees put on a yellow blazer at the induction ceremonies.

566. The correct answer is (A). Yogi Berra is the only member of the Baseball Hall of Fame who hit a World Series pinch-hit grand slam.

567. The correct answer is (C). John Wooden and Lenny Wilkens are both in the Basketball Hall of Fame as a player and as a coach.

568. The correct answer is (B). Vince Lombardi coached the Packers to a 21–17 victory over the Cowboys in the NFL title game.

569. The correct answer is (C). Bart Starr won the game on a quarterback sneak into the end zone.

570. The correct answer is (D). This quote was referring to Wayne Gretzky's record-setting goal on March 23, 1994.

571. The correct answer is (D). Bill Mazeroski's homer over the left field wall gave the Pirates a 10–9 win in the game and a 4–3 win in the World Series.

572. The correct answer is (B). Richard Petty won his 200th race on July 4, 1984, the last win of his career.

573. The correct answer is (C). Magic Johnson's Michigan State Spartans defeated Larry Bird's Indiana State Sycamores in the national championship game.

574. The correct answer is (A). Carlton Fisk waved his homer fair in Game 6 of the 1975 World Series.

575. The correct answer is (B). Evonne Goolagong is the only Aboriginal Australian to become an international tennis star and member of the International Tennis Hall of Fame.

576. The correct answer is (C). Joe Namath guaranteed that his Jets would win Super Bowl III, and he delivered as the Jets beat the Colts 16–7.

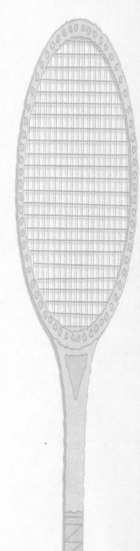

577. The correct answer is (D). John Havlicek, who played with the Boston Celtics from 1962 to 1978, is often considered the best sixth man ever.

578. The correct answer is (A). Pele burst onto the international soccer scene after his performance in the 1958 World Cup. In 1975, Pele came out of retirement and played for the New York Cosmos until 1977.

579. The correct answer is (A). The Chicago Bears, as of 2005, have twenty-six players in the HOF who played all or most of their career with the Bears and five others in the HOF who played at least a little with the Bears.

580. The correct answer is (D). Despite becoming one of the most overpowering starters in MLB history, Nolan Ryan pitched as a reliever during the 1969 World Series.

581. The correct answer is (D). None of the U.S. players have been elected to the Hockey Hall of Fame.

582. The correct answer is (D). Wes Unseld was named MVP and Rookie of the Year in 1969.

583. The correct answer is (C). Chris Evert was the first woman to reach 1,000 singles wins and 150 tournament wins.

584. The correct answer is (A). Ty Cobb coached the Detroit Tigers from 1921 to 1926.

585. The correct answer is (C). Franco Harris caught a ricocheted pass from Terry Bradshaw and ran it in for a score to defeat the Raiders in a playoff game in 1972.

586. The correct answer is (A). Joe Montana found Dwight Clark in the back of the end zone on January 10, 1982, to beat the Cowboys and earn the 49ers a trip to the Super Bowl.

587. The correct answer is (B). Gordie Howe holds the record with 1,767 games played.

588. The correct answer is (C). Willie Mays got his first hit off Warren Spahn in 1951.

589. The correct answer is (D). The Harlem Globetrotters are the most recent team (2002) to be enshrined in the Hall of Fame; there are also four other teams in the Hall.

590. The correct answer is (D). Denis Savard played center for the Blackhawks, Canadiens, and Lightning during his 17-year career.

591. The correct answer is (A). Jimmy Carter was the first boxer to win the world lightweight title three times.

592. The correct answer is (B). Jan Stenerud kicked for the Chiefs, Packers, and Vikings and is the only kicker in the HOF.

593. The correct answer is (C). Harvey Penick was a legendary golf teacher from Texas who taught several other Hall of Famers.

594. The correct answer is (A). Willie Stargell won the MVP award at the age of 39 in 1979.

595. The correct answer is (B). Stan Smith was a dominant Davis Cup player, and he had his own tennis shoes with Adidas.

596. The correct answer is (D). Morgan Wootten coached his way to a 1,210–183 record at DeMatha High School and is the all-time winningest high school coach.

597. The correct answer is (B). Bobby Orr won the Hart, Ross, Norris, and Smythe Trophies during the 1969–70 season.

598. The correct answer is (A). Ted Williams hit a home run in the final at bat of his career on September 28, 1960.

599. The correct answer is (B). O. J. Simpson surpassed the 2,000 yard mark on December 16, 1973.

600. The correct answer is (A). Kareem Abdul-Jabbar retired with 38,387 career points, nearly 7,000 more points than Chamberlain.

601. The correct answer is (D). Jackie Robinson first won the Rookie of the Year Award in 1947 and is now the namesake of the award.

602. The correct answer is (B). Wayne Gretzky won ten Art Ross Trophies and nine Hart Memorial Trophies during his career.

603. The correct answer is (C). Joe Louis got revenge on Schmeling in the 1936 rematch that pitted nation against nation in one of boxing's greatest matches.

604. The correct answer is (B). The trash-talking Bobby Riggs fell to Billie Jean King 6–4, 6–3, 6–3.

605. The correct answer is (B). George Blanda played professional football at the age of 48.

606. The correct answer is (C). Knute Rockne is famous for his "Win one for the Gipper" speech about George Gipp.

607. The correct answer is (A). Johnny Bench was named MVP at the age of 22 in 1970.

608. The correct answer is (C). Gail Goodrich is one of the greatest Lakers to ever play; he also played with the Suns and the Jazz.

609. The correct answer is (A). Zaharias won Olympic gold in hurdles and javelin in the same year she was first introduced to golf.

610. The correct answer is (C). Dick Buttons, along with Michelle Kwan, won the AAU Sulivan award, the top award for amateur athletes.

611. The correct answer is (B). John McEnroe is considered one of the top men's tennis players of all-time and perhaps the greatest lefty ever.

612. The correct answer is (C). Gordie Howe was elected to twelve First Teams and nine Second Teams during his career.

613. The correct answer is (D). Elroy "Crazylegs" Hirsch, Alphonse "Tuffy" Leemans, and Hugh "Shorty" Ray are all in the Pro Football Hall of Fame.

614. The correct answer is (D). Juan Marichal is the only player from the list who never won a Cy Young Award.

615. The correct answer is (A). Boudreau was All-American at the University of Illinois in 1938. He later played for Cleveland and Boston from 1938–1952.

CHAPTER 13

The Sweet Science: Boxing

616. How many different weight divisions are there in boxing?

(A) 10

(B) 13

(C) 17

(D) 27

617. Who is the only father-son combination in the Boxing Hall of Fame?

(A) George and George Foreman

(B) Mike and Arthur Donovan

(C) Muhammad and Laila Ali

(D) Sugar Ray and Justin Leonard

Don't doubt me, because that's when I get stronger.
—MARVIN HAGLER

618. Which of the following describes a boxer in the "Pioneer" category of the Boxing Hall of Fame?

  (A) A fighter who fought before 1892

  (B) A fighter who fought after he was 50 years old

  (C) A fighter who invented a new technique

  (D) A fighter who invented a new piece of boxing equipment

619. Who was the first officially recognized heavyweight champ?

  (A) Jack Dempsey

  (B) Dominick McAffrey

  (C) Rocky Marciano

  (D) John L. Sullivan

620. Who was the oldest boxer to become champion of the world?

  (A) Joe Louis

  (B) Joe Frazier

  (C) Muhammad Ali

  (D) George Foreman

621. Who was the youngest boxer to become champion of the world?

  (A) Sugar Ray Leonard

  (B) Leon Spinks

  (C) Wilfred Benitez

  (D) Sonny Liston

622. Who was the only heavyweight champion to retire with no career losses?

  (A) Rocky Marciano

  (B) Floyd Patterson

  (C) John L. Sullivan

  (D) Evander Holyfield

623. The famous "Rumble in the Jungle" between Ali and Foreman was fought in which of the following countries?

(A) Kenya

(B) Zaire

(C) The Congo

(D) South Africa

624. What body part did Mike Tyson bite off of Evander Holyfield in a fight in 1997?

(A) A lip

(B) A finger

(C) His nose

(D) An ear

625. What famous line did Jack Dempsey give his wife after his loss in the heavyweight title fight in 1926?

(A) "I'm the greatest."

(B) "I pity the fool."

(C) "Honey, I just forgot to duck."

(D) "No mas, no mas."

626. Maxie Rosenbloom earned which of the following nicknames?

(A) "Mighty Maxie"

(B) "Rockin Rosie"

(C) "Marvelous Maxie"

(D) "Slapsie Maxie"

627. How long was the shortest professional boxing match ever?

(A) 5 seconds

(B) 30 seconds

(C) 45 seconds

(D) 1 minute

628. "TKO" is an abbreviation for which of the following?

(A) Total knockout

(B) Technical knockout

(C) Timely knockout

(D) Totally keeled over

629. Who played Rocky Graziano in the movie *Somebody Up There Likes Me*?

(A) Sylvester Stallone

(B) Robert Redford

(C) Robert DeNiro

(D) Paul Newman

630. What boxer held a world title for the longest time?

(A) Muhammad Ali

(B) Sugar Ray Leonard

(C) Lennox Lewis

(D) Joe Louis

631. Marvin Hagler often added which of the following to his name?

(A) "Marvelous"

(B) "Magnanimous"

(C) "Magnificent"

(D) "Malicious"

632. What was Muhammad Ali's name before he changed his name?

(A) Lew Alcindor

(B) Cassius Clay

(C) Chris Jackson

(D) Joe Johnson

633. Who is the only other boxer besides George Foreman to have won a world heavyweight championship and an Olympic gold medal?

   (A) Leo Randolph

   (B) Howard Davis

   (C) Joe Frazier

   (D) Leon Spinks

634. Which of the following weight divisions boasts the lightest boxers?

   (A) Bantamweight

   (B) Junior bantamweight

   (C) Flyweight

   (D) Minimumweight

635. What are the 12 basic rules of boxing known as?

   (A) The Boxing Bylaws

   (B) The Pugilists' Rules

   (C) The Queensbury Rules

   (D) The Kingsbury Rules

636. Where is the International Boxing Hall of Fame?

   (A) Cooperstown, New York

   (B) Canton, Ohio

   (C) Knoxville, Tennessee

   (D) Canastota, New York

637. Who is the only boxer to hold three weight class titles at the same time?

   (A) Muhammad Ali

   (B) Lennox Lewis

   (C) Hank Armstrong

   (D) Oscar de la Hoya

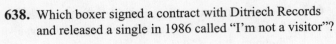

638. Which boxer signed a contract with Ditriech Records and released a single in 1986 called "I'm not a visitor"?

(A) Oscar de la Hoya

(B) Michael Moorer

(C) Hector Camacho

(D) Sugar Ray Leonard

639. Before Mike Tyson pulled his ridiculous antics a few years ago, who did *KO Magazine* list as the dirtiest fighter of all-time?

(A) Gene Fullerm

(B) Jack Dempsey

(C) Tony Galento

(D) Fritzie Zivic

640. Which fighter's opponents gave him the following nicknames: the Mummy, the Octopus, the Ugly Bear, and Dracula?

(A) Rocky Graziano

(B) Muhammad Ali

(C) Mike Tyson

(D) Roberto Duran

641. What boxer holds the record for youngest professional debut?

(A) Teddy Baldock

(B) Jack Dempsey

(C) Jack Johnson

(D) Alberto Arizmendi

642. Who holds the record for most career heavyweight knockouts?

(A) Muhammad Ali

(B) Joe Frazier

(C) Primo Carnera

(D) George Godfrey

643. Which legendary boxer scored at least one knockout in each weight division between flyweight and heavyweight?

(A) Billy Conn

(B) Sonny Liston

(C) Floyd Patterson

(D) Georges Carpentier

644. What was unusual about Al McCoy when he won the middleweight title in 1914?

(A) He was legally blind.

(B) He was the first lefty to win a title.

(C) He was deaf.

(D) He had a wooden leg.

645. U.S. President Gerald Ford coached boxing at what university?

(A) Yale

(B) Harvard

(C) Princeton

(D) Brown

646. Lamar Clark holds the consecutive knockouts record with how many consecutive KO's?

(A) 6

(B) 16

(C) 24

(D) 44

647. Who had the shortest reach of any heavyweight champion?

(A) Rocky Marciano

(B) Larry Holmes

(C) Muhammad Ali

(D) Sonny Liston

648. Which heavyweight champion was knocked down more than any other champ?

(A) Evander Holyfield

(B) Michael Spinks

(C) Floyd Patterson

(D) John L. Sullivan

649. Who shocked the boxing world with a win over heavily-favored Mike Tyson in 1990?

(A) Lennox Lewis

(B) Michael Moorer

(C) Evander Holyfield

(D) Buster Douglas

650. What boxing great defeated Jack Dempsey in 1926 to take the title away from him?

(A) Joe Louis

(B) James Braddock

(C) Gene Tunney

(D) Rocky Marciano

651. Which fighter is often regarded as "the greatest fighter, pound for pound, that ever lived"?

(A) Sugar Ray Robinson

(B) George Foreman

(C) Rocky Graziano

(D) Evander Holyfield

652. Why was Muhammad Ali's boxing title taken away in 1967?

(A) He went to jail for manslaughter.

(B) He converted to Islam.

(C) He refused to enter the draft.

(D) He left the U.S. without a visa.

653. What boxer practically gave up and said "No mas, no mas" in a 1980 fight against Sugar Ray Leonard?

(A) Hector Camacho

(B) Roberto Duran

(C) Oscar de la Hoya

(D) Marvin Hagler

654. Which of the following is the best definition of the term "rope-a-dope"?

(A) A punch that knocks an opponent senseless

(B) A technique that requires boxers to take sense-numbing drugs before each match

(C) A technique where a boxer lays on the ropes, evades his opponent, and thus wears him down

(D) A technique where a boxer beats his opponent against the ropes

655. Who is the only boxer to win a title in five different weight classes?

(A) Sugar Ray Leonard

(B) Sugar Ray Robinson

(C) Floyd Patterson

(D) Hank Armstrong

656. Which of the following is *not* currently a boxing governing body?

(A) The World Boxing Organization

(B) The World Boxing Council

(C) The International Boxing Federation

(D) The Queensbury Boxing Council

657. In the movie series *Rocky*, Rocky Balboa hailed from which of the following cities?

(A) Detroit

(B) The Bronx

(C) Chicago

(D) Philadelphia

212 Sports Questions Your Friends Can't Answer

658. Which two fighters duked it out in the "Thrilla in Manila"?

(A) Ali and Foreman

(B) Ali and Frazier

(C) Frazier and Foreman

(D) Frazier and Liston

659. Which fighter was nicknamed "the Manassa Mauler"?

(A) Joe Louis

(B) Jack Dempsey

(C) John L. Sullivan

(D) Gene Tunney

660. Who defended his heavyweight title a record twenty-five times over a nearly twelve-year stretch?

(A) Jack Britton

(B) John L. Sullivan

(C) Muhammad Ali

(D) Joe Louis

661. Which boxer was known as "Raging Bull"?

(A) Jack LaMotta

(B) Joe Louis

(C) Max Baer

(D) Jack McAuliffe

662. Who holds the record with 42 first-round knockouts?

(A) Jack Dempsey

(B) Gerry Cooney

(C) Jersey Joe Walcott

(D) Young Otto

663. The first in-the-ring fatality in a title bout occurred in which year?

(A) 1897

(B) 1967

(C) 1977

(D) 1987

664. Which famous fighter took a dive in a 1947 fight, a fight that is arguably the most famous fixed fight of all time, in exchange for a title fight at a later date?

(A) Jem Ward

(B) Jake LaMotta

(C) Jack Sharkey

(D) Primo Carnera

665. What strange turn of events took place in a 1997 light heavyweight title fight between Roy Jones Jr. and Montell Griffin?

(A) Both fighters removed their gloves to finish the fight.

(B) The referee was accidentally knocked out twice.

(C) Jones knocked out Griffin but was disqualified for hitting Griffin after he went down, thus giving the title to an unconscious Griffin.

(D) The power went out and Griffin knocked out Jones in the dark.

666. What was controversial about the 1982 WBA heavyweight championship fight between Mike Weaver and Michael Dokes.

(A) Dokes won by disqualification.

(B) Dokes knocked out Weaver with an illegal low blow.

(C) The referee stopped the fight when Weaver was knocked down in the first round, even though Weaver was clearly unhurt.

(D) Weaver was clearly the winner, but lost by decision.

CHAPTER 13 ANSWERS

616. The correct answer is (C). There are seventeen different weight divisions in boxing.

617. The correct answer is (B). The Donovans are the only father/son combo in the Hall of Fame; Mike was a bare-knuckle fighter and Arthur was a referee.

618. The correct answer is (A). A bare-knuckle fighter that fought before 1892 can be inducted into the Boxing Hall of Fame in the Pioneer category.

619. The correct answer is (D). John L. Sullivan knocked out Dominick McAffrey in 1885 to become the first official heavyweight champion.

620. The correct answer is (D). George Foreman was 45 years, 10 months old when he became heavyweight champion in 1994.

621. The correct answer is (C). Wilfred Benitez was only 17 years, 6 months when he won the junior welterweight title in 1976.

622. The correct answer is (A). Rocky Marciano retired with an incredible 49–0 record in 1955.

623. The correct answer is (B). Ali defeated the champ, George Foreman, in Kinshasa, Zaire, in 1974.

624. The correct answer is (D). In one of boxing's strangest episodes ever, Mike Tyson bit off a piece of Evander Holyfield's ear in 1997.

625. The correct answer is (C). Dempsey said, "Honey, I just forgot to duck," to his movie star wife Estelle Taylor.

626. The correct answer is (D). "Slapsie" Maxie Rosenbloom was a weak fighter yet he managed to win many, many fights; most of his wins were by decision.

627. The correct answer is (A). Paul Rees scored a TKO in 5 seconds in a match in Australia in 1991.

628. The correct answer is (B). TKO is short for technical knockout.

629. The correct answer is (D). Paul Newman played Graziano and fighter Tony Zale played himself in the movie.

630. The correct answer is (D). Joe Louis held the heavyweight title for an amazing 11 years, 252 days.

631. The correct answer is (A). "Marvelous" Marvin Hagler was as flashy as his name indicated.

632. The correct answer is (B). Cassius Clay changed his name to Muhammad Ali when he converted to Islam.

633. The correct answer is (C). Joe Frazier won an Olympic gold in 1964 and later won the heavyweight championship.

634. The correct answer is (D). The minimumweight division is for boxers weighing up to 105 pounds.

635. The correct answer is (C). The Queensbury Rules were created in 1867 and named for John Douglas, the Marquess of Queensbury.

636. The correct answer is (D). The International Boxing Hall of Fame is located in Canastota, New York.

637. The correct answer is (C). Hank Armstrong held the featherweight, lightweight, and welterweight titles in 1938.

638. The correct answer is (C). Hector Camacho released the single but very few people bought it.

639. The correct answer is (D). Fritzie Zivic had the dubious honor of being considered the dirtiest fighter of all-time, before Mike Tyson, of course.

640. The correct answer is (B). Now known mostly as "the Champ," Ali was often given nicknames by his opponents.

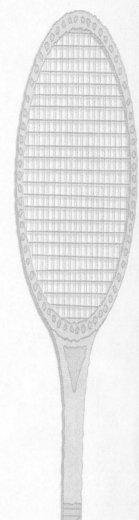

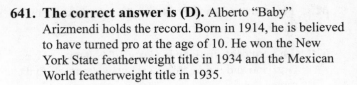

641. **The correct answer is (D).** Alberto "Baby" Arizmendi holds the record. Born in 1914, he is believed to have turned pro at the age of 10. He won the New York State featherweight title in 1934 and the Mexican World featherweight title in 1935.

642. **The correct answer is (D).** George Godfrey scored a record 76 knockouts in his career.

643. **The correct answer is (D).** The Frenchman Georges Carpentier scored a knockout in every weight division from flyweight to heavyweight.

644. **The correct answer is (B).** Al McCoy was the first lefthander to win a world title.

645. **The correct answer is (A).** President Ford coached boxing at Yale University.

646. **The correct answer is (D).** Between 1958 and 1960 Lamar Clark knocked out opponents in 44 consecutive matches.

647. **The correct answer is (A).** Rocky Marciano only had a 68-inch reach, the shortest of any heavyweight champion.

648. **The correct answer is (C).** Floyd Patterson was knocked down twenty times.

649. **The correct answer is (D).** Tyson lost to Buster Douglas, then Douglas lost the title to Holyfield two years later.

650. **The correct answer is (C).** Gene Tunney defeated Jack Dempsey in 1926 to claim the title.

651. **The correct answer is (A).** Sugar Ray Robinson fought more than 200 fights and failed to go the distance just a single time; many boxing authorities consider him one of the greatest fighters of all-time.

652. **The correct answer is (C).** Muhammad Ali refused to enter the draft because war contradicted his Islamic beliefs; therefore, the WBA took away his title.

653. The correct answer is (B). Duran walked away from Leonard in the ring after being frustrated by Leonard.

654. The correct answer is (C). Muhammad Ali first used the "rope-a-dope" technique to defeat George Foreman in the "Rumble in the Jungle."

655. The correct answer is (A). Sugar Ray Leonard won the welterweight in 1979, the junior middleweight in 1981, the middleweight in 1987, and the light heavyweight and super middleweight in 1988.

656. The correct answer is (D). There is no such organization as the Queensbury Boxing Council.

657. The correct answer is (D). Rocky "the Italian Stallion" Balboa grew up and trained in Philadelphia.

658. The correct answer is (B). In 1975, Ali defeated Frazier in Manila when Frazier couldn't make the bell in the fifteenth round.

659. The correct answer is (B). Jack Dempsey earned the nickname "the Manassa Mauler" for the way he mauled his opponents.

660. The correct answer is (D). During his 11-year reign as champion, Joe Louis defended his title, and kept it, an unsurpassed twenty-five times.

661. The correct answer is (A). The nickname "Raging Bull" belonged to the one and only Jack LaMotta.

662. The correct answer is (D). Young Otto scored twelve more first-round knockouts than the next closest fighter.

663. The correct answer is (A). Walter Croots was knocked out in the twentieth round and later died in 1897.

664. The correct answer is (B). Jake LaMotta took a dive against Billy Fox in exchange for a title fight.

665. The correct answer is (C). Jones was indeed disqualified for punching Griffin after he was down and the unconscious Griffin was given the match and the title.

666. The correct answer is (C). The referee stopped the fight in the first round although Weaver was not hurt. In the subsequent match, the bout was declared a draw.

CHAPTER 14

The Ring's the Thing:
Championship Teams

667. Which women's basketball team won the 2002 NCAA basketball championship to become the first women's team to record two undefeated seasons?

(A) Tennessee

(B) UConn

(C) Oklahoma

(D) Old Dominion

668. Which football team won both Super Bowl I and Super Bowl II?

(A) Green Bay Packers

(B) Kansas City Chiefs

(C) Oakland Raiders

(D) Baltimore Colts

The strength of the team is each individual member...
the strength of each member is the team.
—PHIL JACKSON

669. Which team has won the most World Series titles?

   (A) Dodgers

   (B) Giants

   (C) A's

   (D) Yankees

670. During the 1990s, what was the only other state besides Illinois, home of the Chicago Bulls, that produced an NBA champion?

   (A) New York

   (B) Texas

   (C) California

   (D) Florida

671. Which team was the last team to win four consecutive Stanley Cups?

   (A) Detroit Red Wings

   (B) Montreal Canadiens

   (C) Toronto Maple Leafs

   (D) New York Islanders

672. What school shocked the nation when its all-black basketball team beat the great Kentucky team, which was all white, for the NCAA national championship in 1966?

   (A) UCLA

   (B) Duke

   (C) Utah

   (D) UTEP

673. What team won all but one NBA championship between 1959 and 1969?

   (A) Boston Celtics

   (B) Minneapolis Lakers

   (C) Washington Bullets

   (D) Philadelphia Warriors

674. What was the only year since 1904 that there was no World Series winner?

   (A)   1919

   (B)   1945

   (C)   1969

   (D)   1994

675. Which team was the last team to win back-to-back Super Bowls?

   (A)   Dallas Cowboys

   (B)   St. Louis Rams

   (C)   Denver Broncos

   (D)   San Francisco 49ers

676. Which team won the first WNBA championship?

   (A)   L.A. Sparks

   (B)   Houston Comets

   (C)   Utah Starzz

   (D)   Charlotte Sting

677. Which team is the only NBA championship team since the 1985–86 Boston Celtics that did not win at least two consecutive titles?

   (A)   Los Angeles Lakers

   (B)   Detroit Pistons

   (C)   Houston Rockets

   (D)   San Antonio Spurs

678. Which team holds the record for most consecutive World Series championships?

   (A)   New York Yankees

   (B)   Oakland A's

   (C)   Boston Red Sox

   (D)   Detroit Tigers

679. Which team was the last team to win back-to-back NCAA Division I football championships?

(A) Oklahoma

(B) Miami

(C) Nebraska

(D) Florida State

680. Which team defeated the United States 51–50 in a controversial gold medal game in the 1972 Olympic games?

(A) Yugoslavia

(B) The USSR

(C) Mexico

(D) China

681. Which team was the last Canadian team to win the Stanley Cup?

(A) Edmonton Oilers

(B) Calgary Flames

(C) Toronto Maple Leafs

(D) Montreal Canadiens

682. UCLA holds the record for consecutive NCAA basketball championships with how many consecutive titles?

(A) 7

(B) 5

(C) 4

(D) 3

683. What was the first year that the NCAA Division I women's basketball championships were held?

(A) 1902

(B) 1922

(C) 1942

(D) 1982

684. How many times has the World Series been won by a team from outside the United States?

(A) 12

(B) 7

(C) 4

(D) 2

685. How many times has a team won three consecutive Super Bowls?

(A) 0

(B) 1

(C) 2

(D) 3

686. What country has won the World Cup a record four times?

(A) Italy

(B) Brazil

(C) West Germany

(D) France

687. Which team has won the NCAA women's basketball championship a record six times?

(A) UConn

(B) Louisiana Tech

(C) USC

(D) Tennessee

688. How many World Series titles have the Braves won in Atlanta?

(A) 9

(B) 6

(C) 3

(D) 1

689. Which team is the only NCAA Division I football champion to win the national championship despite having two losses?

(A) Alabama

(B) Notre Dame

(C) Minnesota

(D) Ohio State

690. Who is the only team to win the Super Bowl by one point?

(A) New York Giants

(B) New York Jets

(C) New England Patriots

(D) Buffalo Bills

691. Which team was the last team to win back-to-back NCAA men's basketball championships?

(A) Kentucky

(B) UCLA

(C) Duke

(D) Indiana

692. Which team has won the most Stanley Cups?

(A) Montreal Canadiens

(B) Chicago Blackhawks

(C) New York Rangers

(D) Edmonton Oilers

693. Of all the teams that have won at least one World Series title, which team has gone the longest without winning another?

(A) Chicago White Sox

(B) Boston Red Sox

(C) Chicago Cubs

(D) Cleveland Indians

694. Which franchise has won more Super Bowls than any other franchise?

(A) Dallas Cowboys

(B) San Francisco 49ers

(C) Pittsburgh Steelers

(D) Washington Redskins

695. Which of the following teams won the most NBA championships during the 1980s?

(A) Boston Celtics

(B) Detroit Pistons

(C) Los Angeles Lakers

(D) Philadelphia 76ers

696. Which team was the last MLB team to win the World Series in its first World Series appearance?

(A) Florida Marlins

(B) Toronto Blue Jays

(C) Arizona Diamondbacks

(D) Anaheim Angels

697. Which of the following teams needed fourteen wins to claim the NCAA Division I football national championship?

(A) Miami

(B) Oklahoma

(C) Tennessee

(D) No national championship team in Division I has ever won more than 13 games.

698. Which two teams are the only teams to ever win back-to-back NCAA Division I women's basketball championships?

(A) Louisiana Tech and Tennessee

(B) Louisiana Tech and USC

(C) USC and Tennessee

(D) Tennessee and UConn

699. Which team holds the record for the largest margin of victory in the Super Bowl with 45 points?

  (A)   Chicago Bears

  (B)   San Francisco 49ers

  (C)   Dallas Cowboys

  (D)   Green Bay Packers

700. Which team was the last NCAA Division I men's basketball national champion to go undefeated?

  (A)   Duke

  (B)   UCLA

  (C)   Indiana

  (D)   UNLV

701. Which NCAA Division I team has won the College World Series a record 12 times?

  (A)   LSU

  (B)   Southern California

  (C)   Texas

  (D)   Miami

702. For which of the following reasons was there no Stanley Cup champion in 1918–1919?

  (A)   The Stanley Cup series was called off because of war.

  (B)   The Stanley Cup series was called off because the Zamboni broke down.

  (C)   The Stanley Cup series was called off because of a flu outbreak that claimed the life of one of the Stanley Cup finalist's players.

  (D)   The Stanley Cup was stolen.

703. Which of the following cities boasts champions in the
NBA, NHL, NFL, and MLB?

   (A) Atlanta

   (B) Boston

   (C) Los Angeles

   (D) Chicago

704. How many times has a team swept the NBA finals to
become NBA champion?

   (A) 7

   (B) 5

   (C) 3

   (D) 1

705. Which of the following teams, other than the New York
Yankees, have won more than 10 World Series titles?

   (A) Philadelphia/Kansas City/Oakland A's

   (B) St. Louis Cardinals

   (C) Brooklyn/Los Angeles Dodgers

   (D) None of the above

706. Which Super Bowl champion once went four games
during the regular season (their championship season)
without scoring a single offensive touchdown?

   (A) Baltimore Ravens

   (B) New York Giants

   (C) Pittsburgh Steelers

   (D) New York Jets

707. How many times has a team won the World Series
despite one of the Series games ending in a tie?

   (A) 5

   (B) 3

   (C) 2

   (D) 1

708. Which team was the last team to sweep the Stanley Cup Finals?

(A) Colorado Avalanche

(B) New Jersey Devils

(C) Detroit Red Wings

(D) Dallas Stars

709. Which of the following teams committed a record number of penalties in the Super Bowl yet still won the game and the NFL championship?

(A) Green Bay Packers

(B) Baltimore Ravens

(C) New York Giants

(D) Dallas Cowboys

710. Beginning with their first WNBA title, how many consecutive titles did the Houston Comets win before the Los Angeles Sparks took over as champs?

(A) 1

(B) 2

(C) 3

(D) 4

711. Which decade saw the most parity in MLB with nine different teams winning the World Series in ten years?

(A) 1940s

(B) 1950s

(C) 1960s

(D) 1980s

712. In which decade did the fewest number of different teams win the NBA championship?

(A) 1950s

(B) 1960s

(C) 1970s

(D) 1980s

713. Which of the following pairs of teams were the last co-champions in NCAA Division I football?

(A) Miami and Oklahoma

(B) Miami and Virginia Tech

(C) Michigan and Nebraska

(D) Nebraska and Miami

714. Which of the following teams won the first ever NCAA Division I women's basketball championship?

(A) Louisiana Tech

(B) USC

(C) Tennessee

(D) Purdue

715. What Cinderella team emerged as the 1999 Women's World Cup champions after penalty kicks decided the final match?

(A) China

(B) Russia

(C) Jamaica

(D) The United States

716. Which of the following is the only team to win the Super Bowl only to have the Super Bowl MVP award given to a player on the losing team?

(A) Baltimore Colts

(B) New York Jets

(C) New York Giants

(D) San Francisco 49ers

717. Who are the only coaches to play for and coach an NCAA championship team?

(A) Roy Williams ad Bruce Weber

(B) Dean Smith and Bobby Knight

(C) John Thompson and Rollie Massimino

(D) John Wooden and Jim Calhoun

CHAPTER 14 ANSWERS

667. **The correct answer is (B).** UConn went undefeated and won the championship in 2002 and in 1995.

668. **The correct answer is (A).** The Green Bay Packers defeated Kansas City in Super Bowl I and they defeated Oakland in Super Bowl II.

669. **The correct answer is (D).** The Yankees have won a record 26 World Series titles.

670. **The correct answer is (B).** Texas produced the Houston Rockets, who won the title in 1993–94 and 1994–95, and the San Antonio Spurs, who won the title in 1998–99.

671. **The correct answer is (D).** The New York Islanders won four consecutive Stanley Cups between 1980 and 1983.

672. **The correct answer is (D).** Don Haskins led the University of Texas–El Paso to a 72–65 win over heavily favored Kentucky in the 1966 championship game.

673. **The correct answer is (A).** The Celtics won the NBA championship in every year but 1966–67 between 1959 and 1969.

674. **The correct answer is (D).** The World Series was not played in 1994 due to the players' strike that stopped professional baseball.

675. **The correct answer is (C).** The Denver Broncos won Super Bowls XXXII and XXXIII in 1998 and 1999.

676. **The correct answer is (B).** The Houston Comets won the first-ever WNBA championship in 1997.

677. **The correct answer is (D).** The San Antonio Spurs won a single NBA championship in 1998–99.

678. **The correct answer is (A).** The New York Yankees won five consecutive championships between 1949 and 1953.

679. **The correct answer is (C).** The Nebraska Cornhuskers won titles in 1994 and 1995.

680. **The correct answer is (B).** In a game that appeared to be over, time was added to the game clock and the USSR scored a game-winning basket in the extra time to defeat the U.S. team 51–50.

681. **The correct answer is (D).** The Montreal Canadiens won the 1992–93 Stanley Cup. No Canadian team has won the Cup since.

682. **The correct answer is (A).** UCLA won seven consecutive championships from 1967 to 1973.

683. **The correct answer is (D).** The first-ever NCAA Division I women's basketball championship was held in 1982.

684. **The correct answer is (D).** The Toronto Blue Jays are the only non-American team to win the World Series, and they won back-to-back championships in 1992 and 1993.

685. **The correct answer is (A).** No NFL team has ever won three consecutive Super Bowls.

686. **The correct answer is (B).** Brazil won the World Cup in 1958, 1962, 1970, and again in 1994.

687. **The correct answer is (D).** The Tennessee Lady Vols won the championship in 1987, 1989, 1991, 1996, 1997, and 1998.

688. **The correct answer is (D).** The Boston/Milwaukee/Atlanta Braves have won three championships, but the Atlanta Braves only won one championship in 1995.

689. **The correct answer is (C).** Minnesota went 8–2 and still won the national championship in 1960.

690. **The correct answer is (A).** The New York Giants defeated the Buffalo Bills 20–19 in Super Bowl XXV.

691. **The correct answer is (C).** The Duke Blue Devils won back-to-back NCAA basketball championships in 1991 and 1992.

692. **The correct answer is (A).** The Montreal Canadiens have won an astounding twenty-three Stanley Cups.

693. **The correct answer is (C).** The Chicago Cubs haven't won the World Series since 1908.

694. **The correct answer is (B).** The San Francisco 49ers have won all five Super Bowls in which they appeared.

695. **The correct answer is (C).** The Los Angeles Lakers won five NBA championships between 1980 and 1989.

696. **The correct answer is (D).** The Anaheim Angels won the 2002 World Series in their very first World Series appearance.

697. **The correct answer is (D).** Several teams have won the national championship with a record of 13–0, but none have ever won 14 games.

698. **The correct answer is (C).** USC won consecutive titles in 1983 and 1984, and Tennessee won three in a row from 1996 to 1998.

699. **The correct answer is (B).** The San Francisco 49ers beat the Denver Broncos 55–10 in Super Bowl XXIV.

700. **The correct answer is (C).** Indiana went 32–0 in 1976 and won the national championship.

701. **The correct answer is (B).** USC has won twelve College World Series, seven more than the next closest team.

702. **The correct answer is (C).** A flu outbreak killed one of the Montreal Canadiens and the local Health Department called off the series.

703. **The correct answer is (D).** Chicago has produced the NFL champion Bears, the NHL champion Blackhawks, the NBA champion Bulls, and the MLB champion Cubs and White Sox.

704. **The correct answer is (A).** The seven teams are the 2001–02 Lakers, the 1994–95 Houston Rockets, the 1988–89 Detroit Pistons, the 1982–83 Philadelphia 76ers, the 1974–75 Golden State Warriors, the 1970–71 Milwaukee Bucks, and the 1958–59 Boston Celtics.

705. The correct answer is (D). The New York Yankees are the only team to have won more than ten World Series; no other team has won more than nine World Series.

706. The correct answer is (A). The Baltimore Ravens, famous for the terrific defense and anemic offense, went four consecutive games without a single offensive touchdown.

707. The correct answer is (B). The Chicago Cubs won in 1907 with a World Series record of 4–0–1, the Boston Red Sox won in 1912 with a record of 4–3–1 and the New York Giants won in 1922 with a record of 4–0–1.

708. The correct answer is (C). The Red Wings swept the Washington Capitals in the 1997–98 Stanley Cup Finals.

709. The correct answer is (D). The Dallas Cowboys committed 12 penalties in Super Bowl XII yet defeated the Denver Broncos 27–10.

710. The correct answer is (D). The Houston Comets won the first four WNBA titles from 1997 to 2000.

711. The correct answer is (D). The Los Angeles Dodgers were the only two-time champions during the 1980s.

712. The correct answer is (B). During the 1960s, Philadelphia was the only team other than the Boston Celtics to win an NBA title.

713. The correct answer is (C). In 1997, Michigan was ranked number one in the AP poll while Nebraska was ranked number one in the Coaches' poll.

714. The correct answer is (A). Louisiana Tech won the first NCAA Division I women's basketball championship in 1982 by defeating Cheyney 76–62.

715. The correct answer is (D). Brandi Chastain's penalty kick, the U.S. team's fifth and final kick, gave the U.S. team its first ever World Cup in 1999.

716. The correct answer is (A). The Baltimore Colts won Super Bowl V, but the Dallas Cowboys' Chuck Howley was named the Super Bowl MVP.

717. **The correct answer is (B).** Dean Smith played in the 1952 University of Kansas National Championship team and coached the University of North Carolina to two championship titles. Bobby Knight played on the 1960 Ohio State National Championship team and coached Indiana to three national championship titles.

CHAPTER 15

Hanging from the Rafters:
Retired Numbers
(and other famous jersey numbers)

718. What was the original jersey number of Michael Jordan when he played for the Chicago Bulls?

(A) 9

(B) 23

(C) 33

(D) 45

719. What was Michael Jordan's Chicago Bulls jersey number after he came out of retirement the first time?

(A) 9

(B) 23

(C) 33

(D) 45

> I may not shed a tear, but you just don't know the joy I feel inside.
> —PATRICK EWING

720. Which hockey jersey number was shared by Gordie Howe, Maurice Richard, and Bobby Hull?

(A) 1

(B) 4

(C) 9

(D) 21

721. Which baseball great wore the number 7 on his pinstriped jersey?

(A) Mickey Mantle

(B) Roger Maris

(C) Thurman Munson

(D) Reggie Jackson

722. What retired jersey number did Larry Bird wear for the Boston Celtics?

(A) 00

(B) 14

(C) 18

(D) 33

723. Chicago Bears legend Walter "Sweetness" Payton wore which distinguished jersey number?

(A) 24

(B) 34

(C) 44

(D) 45

724. Nolan Ryan had the number 34 jersey retired from which two teams?

(A) Astros and Mets

(B) Angels and Astros

(C) Mets and Angels

(D) Astros and Rangers

725. Nolan Ryan wore the number 30 when he played for which two teams?

(A) Astros and Mets

(B) Angels and Astros

(C) Mets and Angels

(D) Angels and Rangers

726. Which jersey number belonged to "the Great One"?

(A) 99

(B) 88

(C) 77

(D) 6

727. How many Green Bay Packers have retired jersey numbers?

(A) 0

(B) 4

(C) 12

(D) 13

728. The number 32 belonged to what Los Angeles Lakers star?

(A) Wilt Chamberlain

(B) Elgin Baylor

(C) Magic Johnson

(D) Kareem Abdul-Jabbar

729. Which baseball jersey number is arguably the best power-hitting jersey number ever?

(A) 7

(B) 9

(C) 14

(D) 44

730. What jersey number was shared by quarterback greats Terry Bradshaw and Roger Staubach?

   (A) 1

   (B) 7

   (C) 8

   (D) 12

731. How many jersey numbers have the Anaheim Mighty Ducks retired?

   (A) 0

   (B) 1

   (C) 2

   (D) 3

732. What jersey number was shared by Notre Dame quarterbacks Joe Montana, Rick Mirer, and Ron Powlus, but has not been retired?

   (A) 1

   (B) 3

   (C) 7

   (D) 8

733. What jersey number was donned by Cal Ripken Jr., Willie Stargell, Joe Morgan, and Yogi Berra?

   (A) 8

   (B) 16

   (C) 24

   (D) 32

734. If an announcer is to be honored in the same way as a player whose jersey number is retired, what is placed on the announcer's banner in lieu of a jersey number?

   (A) A radio

   (B) A television

   (C) A speaker

   (D) A microphone

735. Sluggers Barry Bonds and Mark McGwire both share which jersey number that will one day be retired and revered?

  (A) 5

  (B) 15

  (C) 25

  (D) 35

736. Which NFL team has retired the most jersey numbers with 13?

  (A) Dallas Cowboys

  (B) San Francisco 49ers

  (C) Chicago Bears

  (D) New York Giants

737. Major League Baseball has retired the number 42 permanently from every major league team to honor which of the following players?

  (A) Jackie Robinson

  (B) Brooks Robinson

  (C) Reggie Jackson

  (D) Babe Ruth

738. How many NFL players have had their jersey retired by more than one team?

  (A) 12

  (B) 8

  (C) 6

  (D) 0

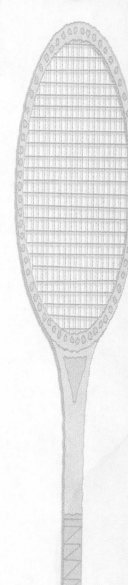

739. Bobby Hull's number 9 jersey has been retired by which two franchises?

    (A) The Chicago Blackhawks and the New York Rangers

    (B) The Detroit Red Wings and the Chicago Blackhawks

    (C) The Phoenix Coyotes and the New York Rangers

    (D) The Chicago Blackhawks and the Phoenix Coyotes

740. The Atlanta Braves' Eddie Mathews' number 41 was retired as which of the following?

    (A) A player

    (B) A coach

    (C) A manager

    (D) A player, coach, and manager

741. Which of the following NFL teams is the only team in the list that has retired a player's number?

    (A) Buffalo Bills

    (B) Oakland Raiders

    (C) Houston Texans

    (D) Jacksonville Jaguars

742. What gritty player's number 34 was retired by the Minnesota Twins in 1997?

    (A) Walter Johnson

    (B) Kirby Puckett

    (C) Rod Carew

    (D) Harmon Killebrew

743. What is the most frequently retired jersey number in the NHL?

    (A) 1

    (B) 2

    (C) 4

    (D) 9

744. Which of the following teams is one of only two NFC teams that has *not* officially retired a player's jersey number?

   (A) Dallas Cowboys

   (B) Tampa Bay Buccaneers

   (C) New Orleans Saints

   (D) Arizona Cardinals

745. Which of the following teams is the only other NFC team that has *not* officially retired a player's jersey number?

   (A) New York Giants

   (B) Atlanta Falcons

   (C) Detroit Lions

   (D) Carolina Panthers

746. Which two MLB teams retired Rod Carew's number 29 jersey?

   (A) Twins and the Rangers

   (B) Angels and the Rangers

   (C) Angels and the Twins

   (D) Twins and A's

747. Maurice and Henri Richard's number 9 and number 16 jerseys, respectively, have been retired by which NHL franchise?

   (A) Calgary Flames

   (B) Montreal Canadiens

   (C) Quebec Nordiques

   (D) Edmonton Oilers

748. What relatively unusual number was retired by the Boston Celtics in honor of "the Chief" Robert Parrish?

   (A) 00

   (B) 0

   (C) 1

   (D) 2

749. What unusual jersey number did the Boston Celtics retire in honor of the great Bill Russell?

(A) 0

(B) 1

(C) 2

(D) 6

750. What baseball legend wore the number 9 jersey, a number now retired by the Boston Red Sox?

(A) Babe Ruth

(B) Carl Yastrzemski

(C) Ted Williams

(D) Carlton Fisk

751. What NFL team retired the 41 jersey to honor Brian Piccolo, a player about whose tragic death was the movie *Brian's Song*?

(A) Detroit Lions

(B) Green Bay Packer

(C) Atlanta Falcons

(D) Chicago Bears

752. Slugger Hank Aaron's number 44 was retired by which two baseball cities because he played for the same franchise in two different cities?

(A) Boston and Atlanta

(B) Boston and Milwaukee

(C) Milwaukee and Kansas City

(D) Milwaukee and Atlanta

753. What jersey number has the Seattle Seahawks organization retired to honor the team's fans?

(A) 1

(B) 12

(C) 100

(D) 99

754. Which of the following teams has retired the most jersey numbers?

   (A) Philadelphia 76ers

   (B) Boston Celtics

   (C) Los Angeles Lakers

   (D) Milwaukee Bucks

755. Joe DiMaggio, Brooks Robinson, Johnny Bench, and George Brett all wore which of the following numbers?

   (A) 2

   (B) 5

   (C) 8

   (D) 13

756. Who is the only professional football player to have his number 19 jersey retired?

   (A) Otto Graham

   (B) Frank Tripucka

   (C) Johnny Unitas

   (D) Bob Griese

757. What jersey number did the Charlotte (now New Orleans) Hornets retire to honor their fans?

   (A) 00

   (B) 0

   (C) 1

   (D) 6

758. What recognizable number is worn by the great Mario Lemieux?

   (A) 66

   (B) 55

   (C) 44

   (D) 33

759. Who had his number 27 retired by the Boston Red Sox and number 72 retired by the Chicago White Sox?

   (A)   Andre Dawson

   (B)   Babe Ruth

   (C)   Harold Baines

   (D)   Carlton Fisk

760. Jerry Sloan, coach of the Utah Jazz, had his number 4 jersey retired by which of the following teams?

   (A)   Utah Jazz

   (B)   Chicago Bulls

   (C)   New York Knicks

   (D)   Atlanta Hawks

761. Which of the following teams has retired the most jersey numbers in MLB history?

   (A)   Boston Red Sox

   (B)   Brooklyn/Los Angeles Dodgers

   (C)   New York Yankees

   (D)   Atlanta Braves

762. Who is the only player to have his number retired by the Washington Redskins?

   (A)   Doug Williams

   (B)   John Riggins

   (C)   Joe Theismann

   (D)   Sammy Baugh

763. What now-retired number did "Pistol" Pete Maravich wear with the Jazz?

   (A)   6

   (B)   7

   (C)   8

   (D)   9

764. Which of the following players is the only other Cubs player besides Ernie Banks to have had his number retired by the Cubs?

(A) Billy Williams

(B) Ryne Sandberg

(C) Hack Wilson

(D) Ron Santo

765. Who is the only player to have his number retired by the Seattle Seahawks?

(A) Jim Zorn

(B) Brian Blades

(C) Steve Largent

(D) Cortez Kennedy

766. What jersey number was retired by the Denver Broncos in honor of John Elway?

(A) 5

(B) 7

(C) 15

(D) 17

767. Which of the following jersey numbers was retired by the Kansas City Chiefs in honor of Len Dawson and is the same number worn by another great Chiefs quarterback while he was with a different team?

(A) 7

(B) 12

(C) 13

(D) 16

CHAPTER 15 ANSWERS

718. **The correct answer is (B).** One of the most famous jersey numbers of all-time, 23 is the number of Jordan's original Chicago Bulls jersey.

719. **The correct answer is (D).** Because Jordan's number 23 jersey had been retired already, Jordan played with 45 on his jersey.

720. **The correct answer is (C).** These three hockey legends all wore 9 on their jerseys.

721. **The correct answer is (A).** Mickey Mantle wore number 7 on his Yankees jersey.

722. **The correct answer is (D).** Larry Bird wore number 33 for the Celtics.

723. **The correct answer is (B).** Payton wore number 34 from 1975 to 1987.

724. **The correct answer is (D).** Nolan Ryan wore number 34 for the Astros and the Rangers.

725. **The correct answer is (C).** Nolan Ryan wore the number 30 for the Mets and the Angels, and the Angels retired the number.

726. **The correct answer is (A).** The number 99 of Wayne Gretzky is one of the most recognizable jerseys in all of sports.

727. **The correct answer is (B).** Only Tony Canadeo, Don Hutson, Bart Starr, and Ray Nitschke have had their numbers retired; the Packers decided in 1983 to discontinue the retirement of numbers.

728. **The correct answer is (C).** The number 32 was retired by the Lakers in honor of Magic Johnson.

729. **The correct answer is (D).** Hank Aaron, Willie McCovey, and Reggie Jackson all wore the number 44.

730. **The correct answer is (D).** Terry Bradshaw wore 12 for the Steelers, and Roger Staubach wore 12 for the Cowboys.

731. The correct answer is (A). The Mighty Ducks have yet to retire a single jersey number.

732. The correct answer is (B). The three great Irish quarterbacks all wore number 3.

733. The correct answer is (A). Each of these baseball legends wore number 8.

734. The correct answer is (D). Announcers are honored with a microphone on a banner; a few examples are Johnny Most of the Boston Celtics and Dave Zinkoff for the Philadelphia 76ers.

735. The correct answer is (C). Bonds and McGwire each wore the number 25 on their uniforms.

736. The correct answer is (C). The Chicago Bears have retired more numbers than any other team, 13.

737. The correct answer is (A). Major League Baseball has officially retired Jackie Robinson's number 42 to honor the roll he played in making baseball an American institution.

738. The correct answer is (D). No NFL player has ever had his jersey retired by more than one team.

739. The correct answer is (D). Bobby Hull's number 9 will never be worn again by a Chicago Blackhawk or by a Phoenix Coyote.

740. The correct answer is (D). Eddie Mathews was a Braves legend as a player, a coach, and a manager.

741. The correct answer is (A). The Buffalo Bills have retired the number 12 jersey of Jim Kelly.

742. The correct answer is (B). Kirby Puckett's number 34 was retired in 1997 in order to honor Puckett's play from 1984 to 1995 with the Twins.

743. The correct answer is (D). The number 9 jersey has been retired eight times in the NHL.

744. The correct answer is (A). The Dallas Cowboys, rather than retiring players' numbers, place the players' names and numbers in their Ring of Honor.

745. The correct answer is (D). The Panthers have a Hall of Honor in which they place players' names and they don't officially retire numbers.

746. The correct answer is (C). The Angels retired Carew's number in 1991, and the Twins retired his number four years earlier.

747. The correct answer is (B). Montreal retired Henri's jersey after twenty years of play and Maurice's jersey after eighteen years of play.

748. The correct answer is (A). "The Chief" made famous the number 00, a seldom used but legal number.

749. The correct answer is (D). Bill Russell wore the number 6. That number is now illegal in high school and college, but not in the pros.

750. The correct answer is (C). The late great Ted Williams wore number 9 for the Boston Red Sox.

751. The correct answer is (D). Brian Piccolo played for the Bears and died tragically of a rare form of cancer, embryonal cell carcinoma in 1970.

752. The correct answer is (D). Hank Aaron played for the Braves in Milwaukee first and then later in Atlanta so both organizations retired his number 44.

753. The correct answer is (B). The Seahawks retired number 12 in honor of their fans, the "twelfth man."

754. The correct answer is (B). The Boston Celtics have retired twenty jersey numbers, more than any other NBA team.

755. The correct answer is (B). Each of these great players wore number 5, making it one of the greatest baseball numbers ever.

756. The correct answer is (C). Johnny Unitas' number 19 jersey is now retired in the Colts organization.

757. The correct answer is (D). The Hornets retired number 6 to honor their sixth man, the fans.

758. The correct answer is (A). Mario Lemieux wears number 66 for the Pittsburgh Penguins.

759. The correct answer is (D). Carlton Fisk was a great player for both the Red Sox and the White Sox.

760. The correct answer is (B). Jerry Sloan was an All-Star player with the Bulls before he entered the coaching ranks.

761. The correct answer is (C). The Yankees have retired the numbers for fifteen different players, coaches, and managers.

762. The correct answer is (D). The Washington Redskins have retired the jersey for only one player, Sammy Baugh who wore number 33.

763. The correct answer is (B). "Pistol" Pete wore number 7 for the New Orleans/Utah Jazz.

764. The correct answer is (A). Billy Williams number 26 is the only number besides Ernie Banks' number 14 to have been retired by the Chicago Cubs.

765. The correct answer is (C). Steve Largent's number 80 is the only player's number that has been retired by the Seahawks.

766. The correct answer is (B). John Elway wore number 7 while playing for the Denver Broncos.

767. The correct answer is (D). Len Dawson wore number 16, Joe Montana also wore number 16, but while he was with the San Francisco 49ers.

My Sports Trivia

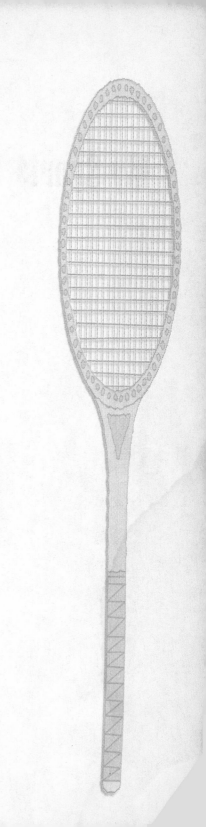

My Sports Trivia

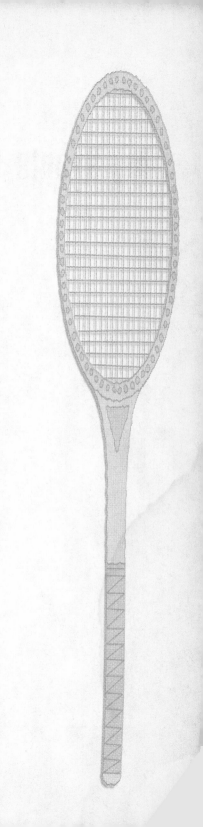

My Sports Trivia